Ecopolis

An Interactive Discovery-Based Social Studies Unit for High-Ability Learners

Grades 6-8

Ecopolis

Richard G. Cote & Darcy O. Blauvelt

PRUFROCK PRESS INC.
WACO, TEXAS

Edited by Sarah Morrison

Production Design by Raquel Trevino

ISBN-13: 978-1-59363-707-1

Prufrock Press Inc.
P.O. Box 8813
Waco, TX 76714-8813
Phone: (800) 998-2208
Fax: (800) 240-0333
http://www.prufrock.com

TABLE OF CONTENTS

Lessons

Introduction

Background

Gifted program directors, resource specialists, and—perhaps most importantly—general education classroom teachers who struggle with the challenge of providing appropriate services to students of high potential in the traditional classroom may be interested in these Interactive Discovery-Based Units for High-Ability Learners. The units encourage students to use nontraditional methods to demonstrate learning.

Any given curriculum is composed of two distinct, though not separate, entities: content and context. In every classroom environment, there are forces at work that define the content to be taught. These forces may take the form of high-stakes tests or local standards. But in these Interactive Discovery-Based Units for High-Ability Learners, the context of a traditional classroom is reconfigured so that students are provided with a platform from which to demonstrate academic performance and understanding that are not shown through traditional paper-and-pencil methods. This way, teachers go home smiling and students go home tired at the end of the school day.

C = C + C
Curriculum = Content + Context

In March of 2005, the Further Steps Forward Project (FSFP) was established and funded under the Jacob K. Javits Gifted and Talented Students Education Program legislation. The project had a two-fold, long-range mission:

- The first goal was to identify, develop, and test identification instruments specific to special populations of the gifted, focusing on the economically disadvantaged.
- The second goal was to create, deliver, and promote professional development focused on minority and underserved populations of the gifted, especially the economically disadvantaged.

The result was the Student Context Rubric (SCR), which is included in each of the series' eight units. The SCR, discussed in further depth in the Appendix, is a rubric that a teacher or specialist uses to evaluate a student in five areas: engagement, creativity, synthesis, interpersonal ability, and verbal communication. When used in conjunction with the units in this series, the SCR provides specialists with an excellent tool for identifying students of masked potential—students who are gifted but are not usually recognized—and it gives general education teachers the language necessary to advocate for these students when making recommendations for gifted and additional services. The SCR also provides any teacher with a tool for monitoring and better understanding student behaviors.

Using best practices from the field of gifted education as a backdrop, we viewed students through the lens of the following core beliefs as we developed each unit:

- instrumentation must be flexible in order to recognize a variety of potentials;
- curricula must exist that benefit all students while also making clear which students would benefit from additional services; and
- identification processes and services provided by gifted programming must be integral to the existing curriculum; general education teachers cannot view interventions and advocacy as optional.

These eight contextually grounded units, two in each of the four core content areas (language arts, social studies, math, and science), were developed to serve as platforms from which middle school students could strut their stuff, displaying their knowledge and learning in practical, fun contexts. Two of the units (*Ecopolis* and *What's Your Opinion?*) were awarded the prestigious National Association for Gifted Children (NAGC) Curriculum Award in 2009. Over the span of 3 years, we—and other general education teachers—taught all of the units multiple times to measure their effectiveness as educational vehicles and to facilitate dynamic professional development experiences.

The FSFP documented that in 11 of 12 cases piloted in the 2008–2009 school year, middle school students showed statistically significant academic gains. In particular, those students who were underperforming in the classroom showed great progress. Furthermore, there were statistically significant improvements in students' perceptions of their classroom environments in terms of innovation and involvement. Finally, the contextually grounded units in this series can be used as springboards for further study and projects, offering teachers opportunities for cross-disciplinary collaboration.

Administrators, teachers, and gifted specialists will gain from this series a better sense of how to develop and use contextualized units—not only in the regular education classroom, but also in gifted programming.

How to Use the Units

Every lesson in the units includes an introductory section listing the concepts covered, suggested materials, grade-level expectations, and student objectives. This section also explains how the lesson is introduced, how students demonstrate recognition of the concepts, how they apply their knowledge, and how they solve related problems. The lesson plans provided, while thorough, also allow for differentiation and adaptation. Depending on how much introduction and review of the material students need, you may find that some lessons take more or less time than described. We have used these units in 50-minute class periods, but the subparts of the lesson—introducing the material, recognizing the concepts, applying knowledge, and solving a problem—allow for adaptability in terms of scheduling. The "Additional Notes" for each lesson provide further tips, flag potential problem areas, and offer suggestions for extending the lesson.

This series offers many contextual units from which to choose; however, we do not recommend using them exclusively. In our research, we have found that students who are constantly involved in contextual learning become immune to its benefits. We recommend, therefore, that you vary the delivery style of material across the school year. For most classes, spacing out three contextual units over the course of the year produces optimal results.

These units may be used in place of other curriculum. However, if you find that your students are stumbling over a specific skill as they progress through a unit, do not hesitate to take a day off from the unit and instead use direct instruction to teach that skill. This will help to ensure that students are successful as they move forward. It is necessary for students to be frustrated and challenged, as this frustration serves as the impetus of learning—yet they must not be so frustrated that they give up. Throughout the unit, you must find the delicate balance between providing challenges for your students and overwhelming them.

The Role of the Teacher

A contextual unit is a useful vehicle both for engaging your students and for assessing their abilities. As a teacher, your role changes in a contextual unit. Rather than being the driving force, you are the behind-the-scenes producer. The students are the drivers of this creative vehicle. If you are used to direct instruction methods of teaching, you will need to make a conscious choice not to run the show. Although this may feel a bit uncomfortable for you in the beginning, the rewards for your students will prove well worth the effort. As you become more comfortable with the process, you will find that this teaching method is conducive to heightening student engagement and learning while also allowing you to step back and observe your students at work.

Group Dynamics

Cooperation plays a key role in this unit. Small-group work is fraught with challenges for all of us. Creating groups that will be able to accomplish their objectives—groups whose members will fulfill their roles—takes some forethought. Keep in mind that sometimes the very act of working through any issues that arise may be the most powerful learning tool of all. Before beginning the unit, you should discuss with students the importance of working together and assigning tasks to ensure that work is distributed and completed fairly and equally.

Preparation and Pacing

Deciding on a timeline is very important as you plan the implementation of the unit. You know your students better than anyone else does. Some students may be more successful when they are immersed in the unit, running it every day for 3 weeks. Others would benefit from having some days off to get the most out of their experiences.

Every classroom is different. Students possess different sets of prior knowledge, learning strategies, and patterns. This means that as the teacher, you must make decisions about how much of the material you will introduce prior to the unit, whether you will provide occasional traditional instruction throughout the unit, how many days off you will give students, and how much your students will discover on their own throughout the course of the unit. For example, in this social studies unit, students participate in a simulation that involves the concepts of scarcity, resource allocation, and taxation in a market economy. You may choose to teach these concepts prior to using the unit, and then use the unit to replace the practice days that would usually follow. Another option is to use the unit without preteaching these concepts, instead allowing the unit's activities to show which students already possess some content knowledge and which students are experiencing more difficulty. If you choose the latter option, it is important to use the pretest carefully and to cultivate an encouraging atmosphere in the classroom. This book is not meant to provide exact instructions; in every lesson, there is wiggle room in terms of how you work alongside students to enable them to demonstrate learning.

Also, you should feel free to use materials other than those suggested. If there is a topic or source that is highly relevant for your students, then it might be worthwhile for you to compile research sites, articles, and other materials about the topic in order to provide your students a degree of real-world involvement.

Using these units is a bit like using a recipe in the kitchen. The first time you use one of the units, you may want to use it just as it is written. Each successive time you use it, however, you may choose to adjust the ratios and substitute ingredients to suit your own tastes. The more you personalize the units to your students' situations and preferences, the more engaged they will be—and the same goes for you as the teacher.

Grade-Level Expectations

All of our units are aligned with New Hampshire's Grade-Level Expectations. These state requirements are similar to many states' GLEs, and we hope that they will be useful for you. For each lesson, we have listed the applicable New Hampshire GLEs in a format that illustrates which learning objectives students are meeting by completing the given tasks.

Adaptability

"Organized chaos" is a phrase often used to describe a contextual classroom. The students are not sitting at their desks and quietly taking notes while the teacher delivers information verbally. A classroom full of students actively engaged in their learning and creatively solving real-world problems is messy, but highly productive. Every teacher has his or her own level of tolerance for this type of chaos, and you may find yourself needing days off occasionally. Organization is an essential ingredient for success in a contextual unit. For example, you will need a place in your classroom where students can access paperwork. It is important to think through timeframes and allow for regular debriefing sessions.

You will also want to develop a personalized method for keeping track of who is doing what. Some students will be engaged from the start, but others you will need to prod and encourage to become involved. This will be especially true if your students are unfamiliar with this type of contextual learning. There are always a few students who try to become invisible so that classmates will do their work for them. Others may be Tom Sawyers, demonstrating their interpersonal skills by persuading peers to complete their work. You will want to keep tabs on both of these types of students so that you can maximize individual student learning. Some teachers have students keep journals, others use daily exit card strategies, and others use checklists. Again, many aspects of how to use these units are up to you.

It is difficult in a busy classroom to collect detailed behavioral data about your students, but one advantage of contextual learning is that it is much easier to spend observation time in the classroom when you are not directly running the show! If you have the luxury of having an assistant or classroom visitor who can help you collect anecdotal data, then we recommend keeping some sort of log of student behavior. What has worked well for us has been to create a list of students' pictures, with a blank box next to each picture in which behaviors can be recorded.

Contextual units require the teacher to do a considerable amount of work prior to beginning the unit, but once you have put everything into place, the students take over and you can step back and observe as they work, solve problems, and learn.

Unit Overview

The tasks in this unit are designed to assess the degree to which students understand and apply economic concepts including needs and wants, opportunity costs, entrepreneurship, allocation of resources (scarcity and abundance), and global interdependence. Lessons 1–4 make up the preparation component of the unit. During these lessons, teachers implement a system whereby students earn capital for their savings accounts in various ways: completing homework on time, doing well on tests, performing random acts of kindness, and so forth.

Students then put this capital to work in the simulated economy of Ecopolis, in which students play elected officials, bankers, and consumers. (The leader is called the Head Honcho, the assistant leader is called the Big Deal, the treasury chairperson and tax collector is called Deep Pockets, the bankers are called Money Bags, and consumers are called John Q. and Jane Q. Public. Together, they are Ecopolitans, the citizens of this government.) Students work toward the goal of buying preferred seating, although you may choose to adapt the unit and use different incentives for students. In the final portion of the unit, students have to work together to recover from an economy-impacting event, and they conclude the unit by demonstrating what they have learned through one-on-one interviews.

This unit is intended to challenge all students. When you are assigning roles, you will want to consider students' scores on the Economics Preassessment and the

Banker Selection Qualifier as well as their levels of maturity and ability. Different roles require different skills; however, every role can challenge a student, regardless of his or her abilities. For instance, a highly able student could excel as an elected official, a banker, or a consumer.

The consumers make up the engine of this interactive unit, powering the simulation. The elected officials are the engineers who drive the train by enacting laws and policies for the city of Ecopolis that benefit all Ecopolitans. The bankers are responsible for keeping accounts in order and making it financially possible for consumers to achieve their goals. Simply put, students' roles depend just as much on maturity, temperament, and spirit of cooperation as they do on ability (although ability is also important).

Each lesson is subdivided to give you more latitude in differentiating based on students' prior knowledge, skills, levels of engagement, and readiness. It is left to you, as the teacher, to determine a starting point for each student.

The unit contains five distinct assessment tools for student evaluation. The Student Context Rubric in the Appendix can be used throughout the unit to catalogue student behaviors that demonstrate hidden potential. The Economics Preassessment provided in Lesson 1 is administered again in Lesson 8 as an Economics Postassessment. The Banker Selection Qualifier, in addition to informing your decisions about role assignments, is also used to measure students' mathematical progress. Finally, the Complete the Statements sheet included in Lesson 8 measures content knowledge, and a final interview serves as an interactive evaluation for each student. Thus, the breadth and depth of the provided assessment tools allow teachers to gain in-depth understanding of students' learning processes.

Unit Outline

We designed these lessons to be used during 50-minute class periods. Depending on the extent to which you need to review concepts with your students, and the amount of time you decide to devote to particular activities, some of these lessons may take fewer or more days than indicated. We have tried to note how many days each lesson will take to complete.

In the days leading up to the unit, you will want to implement a system by which students can earn capital. Students can earn money by completing their homework on time, for instance, or through doing volunteer work. (This is explained further in the Additional Notes section of Lesson 1.) You will also want to give students a basic idea of what they will be doing and what the major roles of the simulation will be. Explain to them that they will be running their own economic system, called Ecopolis, and that some of them will serve as bankers and elected officials.

Lesson 1

Students complete the Economics Preassessment and the Banker Selection Qualifier, preassessment materials that will help you decide which students should play which roles in the simulated government of Ecopolis. Students who display exceptional math skills should be assigned roles as bankers. After a discussion of the elements of effective public speaking and marketing strategies, students are given an assignment requiring them to launch marketing campaigns for fictional products. (Not only will this give them an increased understanding of concepts such as factors of production, but it will also assist you in deciding which students will be candidates for elected official positions.) Students spend the first day of this lesson completing preassessment activities and preparing sales pitches; on the second day, students deliver their sales pitches, which you assess using the provided rubric. (*Note:* This lesson requires 2 days.)

Lesson 2

Students are introduced to the concepts of Ecopolis, the interactive roles, and the object of the simulation. Students are also given folders (or they can bring them in), which will serve as journals that they will maintain throughout the unit to document their understanding and progress. They will also have a considerable amount of paperwork, which they should keep in their folders. They will need their forms to pay taxes, document their earnings, and complete other functions; they will also need proof of their accomplishments at the end of the unit. Based on students' performance on preassessment activities, as well as on other factors, students are assigned roles as bankers, political candidates, and campaign managers.

Lesson 3

Role descriptions are discussed. The class is then subdivided into four groups: Money Bags (bankers), candidates to be the Head Honcho (leader), candidates to be the Big Deal (assistant leader), and candidates to be Deep Pockets (the treasury chairperson/tax collector). Each political candidate is also assigned a campaign manager. Bankers are given a banker tutorial, which takes 2 days to complete and which gives them an understanding of the forms they will be using in the simulation. Each group of candidates and campaign managers (for the Head Honcho, the Big Deal, and Deep Pockets positions) is assigned a different issue, and each candidate-manager pair spends 2 days researching, writing, and practicing a speech that will teach their classmates about the issue (and hopefully get them elected!). (*Note:* This lesson requires 2 days.)

Lesson 4

The students review the elements of effective public speaking. The bankers present the information that they learned in the banker tutorial, which will help students understand how they will conduct their financial transactions in the simulation. Then, each candidate makes a speech on the issue that he or she has researched. You may choose to allow campaign managers to speak in some capacity as well (e.g., answer questions following candidates' speeches). The polls are opened, and everybody votes.

Lesson 5A

Election results are announced, and roles and responsibilities are reviewed. Elected officials receive their job description prompts and their salaries, and they inform the Ecopolitans of their visions for Ecopolis. Consumers receive their job description prompts and form strategies to earn capital. Students create savings accounts and proceed to Deep Pockets to pay taxes. Stipends of $500 are paid to Ecopolitans who have earned less than $1,000; these stipends come from the $10,000 one-time payment made to the government by the Ecomaster. (*Note:* This lesson requires at least 2 days.)

Lesson 5B

This supplemental lesson is provided in case students playing the roles of elected officials find themselves with little to do as their fellow Ecopolitans and bankers are busy with transactions. The Head Honcho, the Big Deal, and Deep Pockets are given assignments for speeches that they will have to make before receiving their second salary payments in Lesson 7. (These salary payments will come from collected tax money.) Elected officials may begin preparing for these speeches in class—which will cover, respectively, the issues of resource allocation, wants vs. needs, and taxation in a market economy. They may continue researching and preparing both in class (when they have spare time) and outside of class.

Lesson 6

Taxes continue to be collected as money is made. Students propose jobs, goods, and services in order to earn capital. Banks continue to run. The last 10–15 minutes of class is reserved for debriefing, so that students can reflect on how the day went and consider what they might do differently the following day. Also, students can think collectively about how to address any issues that surface in the simulation. Students are encouraged to think outside of the box: If they are unhappy about not being able to afford preferred seating, then what marketable services could they offer? This stage of the unit can be run for as long as students are actively engaged in running their simulated economy, but we suggest 2 days as a minimum. Once the students are reasonably comfortable with their roles in Ecopolis, they will receive an issue of *The Rug Tug Times* (Ecopolis's newspaper) informing them that elected officials will be making speeches on issues that, by this point, they will likely be interested in—such as why taxes are so high. (*Note:* This lesson requires at least 2 days.)

Lesson 7

At the beginning of the class period, elected officials make speeches on the topics they were assigned in Lesson 5B. Following their speeches, they receive their second salary payments, funded by tax dollars. After this, a crisis edition of *The Rug Tug Times* is distributed describing a situation that will force the economy to change significantly. Students will realize that global interdependence has resulted in an outflow of money from Ecopolis. The provided issue of *The Rug Tug Times* addresses the issue of global interdependence. The students must then brainstorm and implement ways to rebalance their economy.

Lesson 8

The students are informed that a reassessment process will begin in a few days. Students will go through interviews wherein they provide evidence (including their journals and accounting records) of what they have learned. We recommend that students prepare visual aids for their interviews. If you wish, you can allow students to have reelections at this point and then continue running the simulation. (*Note:* This lesson requires 2 days.)

Glossary of Terms

For the purposes of this unit, the following definitions will be used.

- **Big Deal:** assistant to Head Honcho; serves as liaison between Head Honcho and consumers
- **Capitalism:** economic system in which property is privately owned and goods are privately produced; sometimes referred to as the private enterprise system
- **Competition:** condition wherein there are many buyers and sellers, making it impossible for individual consumers to impact prices
- **Consumer:** person who buys economic goods and services
- **Credit:** giving a person goods and services in return for the promise of payment at a future time; payment usually bears interest
- **Deep Pockets:** treasury chairperson of Ecopolis
- **Demand:** the quantity of an item, per unit of time, that buyers are willing to buy at varying costs
- **Deposit:** to put money into a bank or other financial institution
- **Distribution:** the channels and incentives that play a role in delivering a product to customers

- **Economics:** the study of choice and decision making in a world with limited resources
- **Ecopolitans:** the students participating, as citizens, in the simulated economy of Ecopolis
- **Export:** to send or sell goods and services to foreign countries
- **Factors of Production:** the mix of resources chosen to make and distribute a product
- **Global Interdependence:** the impact that foreign economies have on domestic ones
- **Goods:** often called "goods and services"; an encompassing term meaning options, products, labor, and other materials that people want and for which they will pay
- **Head Honcho:** leader of Ecopolis
- **Import:** to bring in or buy goods or services from a foreign country
- **Income:** the amount of money one earns, whether through a job, investments, or another source
- **Inflation:** increase in the overall level of prices over an extended period of time
- **Interdependence:** people's or businesses' reliance on other people or businesses to help each other
- **Invest:** to commit money or capital in order to gain financial returns later on; to put one's money or resources into a business or project with the expectation of gaining money back
- **Manufacture:** to make or process a raw material into a finished product, especially by means of a large-scale industrial operation
- **Money Bags:** bankers in the simulated economy of Ecopolis
- **Needs:** resources that are required for survival
- **Promotion:** advertising, packaging, and other strategies that are used to attract customers to a product
- **Resources:** ingredients, including labor resources and capital, that are available to produce goods and generate services
- **Scarcity:** the condition where there are too few resources to satisfy human wants; the most basic economic concept
- **Supply:** the various quantities per unit of time that are sold at various prices
- **Surplus:** when the quantity of a supplied good exceeds the quantity demanded of that good at the existing price
- **Tariff:** a tax on imports
- **Tax:** a required contribution by persons, groups, or businesses made to support the government; types include income, sales, state, local, and federal
- **Wants:** the various desires of human beings that provide the driving force of economic activity; economics dictates that people will always have wants

Lesson 1

Concepts

- Factors of production
- Product price determination
- Marketing (product, price, place, and promotion)
- Elements of effective public speaking

Materials

- Banker Selection Qualifier sheet (pp. 18–19; answer key on pp. 20–21)
- Economics Preassessment sheet (pp. 22–23; answer key on pp. 24–25)
- Product Overview sheets A, B, and C (pp. 26–28)
- Sales pitch presentation rubric (p. 29)
- Earnings Statement sheet (p. 30)

Student Objective

The student completes preassessment activities to help determine his or her role in Ecopolis.

Introduction

In the days leading up to the unit, give the students an overview of what they will be doing (i.e., running their own economy and filling various positions in that economy). Students may be given opportunities to earn capital in various ways (see Additional Notes). All students complete the Banker Selection Qualifier. Inform students that this qualifier may ask about topics that have not been addressed in class, and that the qualifier is not for a grade, but may be used to help determine their roles in Ecopolis. Students also complete the Economics Preassessment. Introduce the concepts of powerful public speaking and marketing's "Four P's,"—

product, price, place, and promotion—and announce that students with successful sales pitches may be selected to run for office.

Recognition

Through dialogue, students demonstrate an understanding of marketing and public speaking concepts.

Application

Students use the provided materials to understand marketing concepts and develop strategies.

1. Give students overview sheets for Products A, B, or C, or allow them to invent their own products, making sure that they focus on the same marketing concepts.
2. Review the directions on each sheet.
3. Review the presentation rubric. Discuss the concepts of eye contact, projection, enunciation, tempo, and organization.
4. Have students develop sales pitches and speeches using the provided guidelines and whatever information you choose to provide regarding marketing techniques.

Problem Solving

On the second day of this lesson, students use the concepts they have learned about public speaking and marketing.

1. Each student gives a 1-minute sales pitch for Product A, B, or C.
2. Use the provided rubric to assess each student's sales pitch.

Grade-Level Expectations

The student:

• Identifies the role of the individual in factors of production and markets.
• Understands and identifies resources, entrepreneurship, human resources, capital resources, and natural resources.

Additional Notes

• In the days leading up to this unit, we suggest that you encourage students to earn money to use as a medium of exchange during Ecopolis. The Earnings Statement sheet on page 30 is a form that students can use to keep track of their finances before and during the unit. You should keep matching records to ensure that students' records are correct. In the days leading up to the unit, students can earn money from a posted or distributed list of behaviors.

Which behaviors you decide to reward will be up to you (because classrooms are so varied with regard to behaviors, schedules, and rules, we have not provided concrete guidelines). However, here are some possibilities that have worked well for us:

o Homework handed in on time: $100

o Earning an A on a quiz or test: $500

o Completing an extra credit assignment: $350

o Doing a favor for the teacher or a classmate: $200–$400

o Community service work (e.g., picking up litter in the schoolyard): $100–$500

We recommend that you set prices in order to allow at least some students to earn around $4,000. For Ecopolis to function properly, some students need to have at least $3,500. (This will enable several students to buy preferred seating, provided that they have additional assistance in the form of loans from the bank.)

- Because bankers will be handling other students' money and will be under a considerable amount of pressure, it is important to assign this role only to students who are capable of performing it and will not become overly stressed by their responsibilities. The Banker Selection Qualifier should help you determine which students possess the necessary skills; additionally, bankers should be able to multitask, have excellent communication skills, and be fairly outgoing.

- The sales pitch activity is designed to assist you in selecting candidates for the offices of Head Honcho (leader), Big Deal (assistant to the leader), and Deep Pockets (the tax collector or treasury chairperson). The economy's leaders must be excellent communicators, but—just as in real life—they do not necessarily need to possess the most economic knowledge.

- The provided rubric highlights talents necessary for leadership and public speaking. This assessment will inform your decisions regarding which students should be assigned roles either as candidates for political office or as campaign managers. Depending on how much time you have, you may want to have a more in-depth discussion of the elements of successful public speaking and marketing, particularly the four P's. It is up to you how much time to spend on these concepts.

BANKER SELECTION QUALIFIER

Place your answers to the following questions in the boxes on the right.

1. To find the percentage of change, divide the actual change in value by the original number.
    A. True
    B. False

2. 60% of 75 is
    A. 2.5
    B. 45
    C. 450
    D. 125

3. 50 is _____ % of 80.
    A. 1.6
    B. .625
    C. 62.5
    D. 160

4. If your income in 2010 was $20,000 a year, and your income grew to $25,000 a year in 2011, then it has grown by:
    A. 25%
    B. 20%
    C. 1.25%
    D. 80%

5. In the formula I = P x R x T, I represents interest, P represents principal, R represents rate, and T represents time. If you borrowed $8,000 (the principal) at an interest rate of 9% (the rate) for 1 year (the time), then much interest would you be charged?
    A. $9,300
    B. Not enough information is provided.
    C. $888.89
    D. $720

6. Charlie borrowed $100 from Martha to buy a Wii. Charlie agreed to pay Martha back $110. How much interest did Charlie pay?
    A. $10
    B. $110
    C. $90
    D. $100

7. In problem 6, what was the interest rate Charlie paid to get the loan (assume 1 for the time)?
   A. 100%
   B. 10%
   C. 5%
   D. 110%

8. On a line graph, a positive, linear change is shown by:
   A. A straight line moving up when going to the right.
   B. A straight line moving down when going to the right.
   C. A curved line moving down when going to the right.
   D. A curved line moving up when going to the right.

9. On a graph, the x-axis is:
   A. The horizontal axis.
   B. The vertical axis.
   C. The axis of rotation.
   D. The pivot point of the graph.

10. Study the graph shown below.

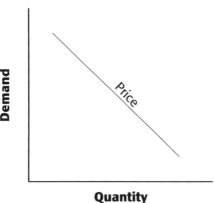

The graph shows that:
   A. As price decreases, the quantity demanded increases.
   B. As price increases, the quantity demanded increases.
   C. The richer people become, the more they buy.
   D. People who are poor pay lower prices for goods.

Ecopolis © Prufrock Press Inc.

Permission is granted to photocopy or reproduce this page for single classroom use only.

19

BANKER SELECTION QUALIFIER
ANSWER KEY

1. To find the percentage of change, divide the actual change in value by the original number.
   A. True
   B. False

A

2. 60% of 75 is
   A. 2.5
   B. 45
   C. 450
   D. 125

B

3. 50 is _____ % of 80.
   A. 1.6
   B. .625
   C. 62.5
   D. 160

C

4. If your income in 2010 was $20,000 a year, and your income grew to $25,000 a year in 2011, then it has grown by:
   A. 25%
   B. 20%
   C. 1.25%
   D. 80%

A

5. In the formula I = P x R x T, I represents interest, P represents principal, R represents rate, and T represents time. If you borrowed $8,000 (the principal) at an interest rate of 9% (the rate) for 1 year (the time), then much interest would you be charged?
   A. $9,300
   B. Not enough information is provided.
   C. $888.89
   D. $720

D

6. Charlie borrowed $100 from Martha to buy a Wii. Charlie agreed to pay Martha back $110. How much interest did Charlie pay?
   A. $10
   B. $110
   C. $90
   D. $100

A

7. In problem 6, what was the interest rate Charlie paid to get the loan (assume 1 for the time)?
    A. 100%
    B. 10%
    C. 5%
    D. 110%

8. On a line graph, a positive, linear change is shown by:
    A. A straight line moving up when going to the right.
    B. A straight line moving down when going to the right.
    C. A curved line moving down when going to the right.
    D. A curved line moving up when going to the right.

9. On a graph, the x-axis is:
    A. The horizontal axis.
    B. The vertical axis.
    C. The axis of rotation.
    D. The pivot point of the graph.

10. Study the graph shown below.

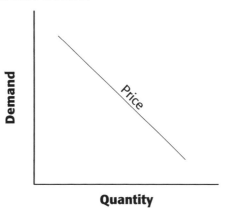

The graph shows that:
    A. As price decreases, the quantity demanded increases.
    B. As price increases, the quantity demanded increases.
    C. The richer people become, the more they buy.
    D. People who are poor pay lower prices for goods.

ECONOMICS PREASSESSMENT

Place your answers to the following questions in the boxes on the right.

1. Economics is the study of:
   A. How to produce goods.
   B. How to make decisions on spending.
   C. How society decides what, how, and for whom to produce goods and services.
   D. How to run our country.

2. Economic resources are:
   A. Things like water and clean air.
   B. Items available for producing goods that satisfy human wants.
   C. Dependent on tastes and preferences of the population.
   D. The living standard in our society.

3. A basic economic problem is that resources are:
   A. Too expensive.
   B. Able to be used for many things.
   C. Able to be combined to produce a commodity.
   D. Scarce.

4. In a free market economy:
   A. Prices adjust upward or downward depending on how scarce goods are.
   B. The government decides how much goods will cost.
   C. The government decides which goods will be produced.
   D. Free goods are given away at the supermarket.

5. The opportunity cost of a good is:
   A. The value of something else that is passed up when a good or service is bought.
   B. The amount of money spent on a product.
   C. The interest we get at a bank.
   D. The amount of time we spend shopping.

6.   When two goods can be used for the same purpose, they are
     said to be:
     A. A good bargain.
     B. Good for the economy.
     C. In demand.
     D. Substitutes.

7.   The demand for a good can change if:
     A. I get a raise.
     B. The price of everything else goes up.
     C. There is a change in consumers' tastes and preferences.
     D. All of the above.

8.   To economize means to:
     A. Study economics.
     B. Do the best you can with what you have.
     C. Save as much money as possible.
     D. Not buy anything.

9.   On a graph, the demand curve:
     A. Moves downward as it goes to the right.
     B. Is the vertical axis.
     C. Moves upward as it goes to the right.
     D. Usually appears in red.

10. A characteristic of economic "wants" is that:
     A. They are necessary for existence.
     B. They are the same in all cultures.
     C. They can never be fully satisfied.
     D. They can be classified as labor or capital.

ECONOMICS PREASSESSMENT/ POSTASSESSMENT
ANSWER KEY

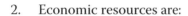

1. Economics is the study of:
    A. How to produce goods.
    B. How to make decisions on spending.
    C. How society decides what, how, and for whom to produce goods and services.
    D. How to run our country.

2. Economic resources are:
    A. Things like water and clean air.
    B. Items available for producing goods that satisfy human wants.
    C. Dependent on tastes and preferences of the population.
    D. The living standard in our society.

3. A basic economic problem is that resources are:
    A. Too expensive.
    B. Able to be used for many things.
    C. Able to be combined to produce a commodity.
    D. Scarce.

4. In a free market economy:
    A. Prices adjust upward or downward depending on how scarce goods are.
    B. The government decides how much goods will cost.
    C. The government decides which goods will be produced.
    D. Free goods are given away at the supermarket.

5. The opportunity cost of a good is:
    A. The value of something else that is passed up when a good or service is bought.
    B. The amount of money spent on a product.
    C. The interest we get at a bank.
    D. The amount of time we spend shopping.

6. When two goods can be used for the same purpose, they are said to be:
   A. A good bargain.
   B. Good for the economy.
   C. In demand.
   D. Substitutes.

7. The demand for a good can change if:
   A. I get a raise.
   B. The price of everything else goes up.
   C. There is a change in consumers' tastes and preferences.
   D. All of the above.

8. To economize means to:
   A. Study economics.
   B. Do the best you can with what you have.
   C. Save as much money as possible.
   D. Not buy anything.

9. On a graph, the demand curve:
   A. Moves downward as it goes to the right.
   B. Is the vertical axis.
   C. Moves upward as it goes to the right.
   D. Usually appears in red.

10. A characteristic of economic "wants" is that:
    A. They are necessary for existence.
    B. They are the same in all cultures.
    C. They can never be fully satisfied.
    D. They can be classified as labor or capital.

PRODUCT A

Congratulations! You have been asked to create a marketing pitch for our new product. We have included a description of the product, its intended purpose, and the cost of producing this product. You must name the product, determine additional uses for the product, and set a price—based on the given production costs—that will allow the company to make a profit. (Remember, if the price is too high, people will not buy your product, even if your sales pitch is great!)

Description: This new electrical wonder is able to create a solid sphere with whatever material is placed into its base. The material is inserted into the base, and after the user carefully seals the opening, the power is turned on. Centripetal force pulls the material into the bulb, where it develops into a solid sphere. When the process is complete, the device stops spinning, and the bulb pops open and spits out a new sphere.

Factors of Production:
Materials: $5.87
Labor: $9.53
Packaging: $1.35
Total: $16.75

Tomorrow, you will deliver a 1-minute sales pitch for this product. Be as convincing and persuasive as possible, because your goal is to make everyone in the room want to go out and buy this product. Remember to include a name for the product, a brief description of it, an explanation of its purpose, and how much it costs.

PRODUCT B

Congratulations! You have been asked to create a marketing pitch for our new product. We have included a description of the product, its intended purpose, and the cost of producing this product. You must name the product, determine additional uses for the product, and set a price—based on the given production costs—that will allow the company to make a profit. (Remember, if the price is too high, people will not buy your product, even if your sales pitch is great!)

Description: This new wonder allows the creative cook to invent many new recipes. The high-powered blender will analyze any combination of food products and let the operator know if the ingredients taste good together. A red light will blink if the newly added ingredients are incompatible, and a suggestion on how to fix the problem will print out. The user simply adds the ingredients into the top and turns on the power. When the new food product is ready, the machine turns off automatically. To access the new creation, the user opens the spigot at the bottom of the machine.

Factors of Production:
Materials: $9.71
Labor: $23.86
Packaging: $5.92
Total: $39.49

Tomorrow, you will deliver a 1-minute sales pitch for this product. Be as convincing and persuasive as possible, because your goal is to make everyone in the room want to go out and buy this product. Remember to include a name for the product, a brief description of it, an explanation of its purpose, and how much it costs.

Ecopolis © Prufrock Press Inc.

27

Permission is granted to photocopy or reproduce this page for single classroom use only.

PRODUCT C

Congratulations! You have been asked to create a marketing pitch for our new product. We have included a description of the product, its intended purpose, and the cost of producing this product. You must name the product, determine additional uses for the product, and set a price—based on the given production costs—that will allow the company to make a profit. (Remember, if the price is too high, people will not buy your product, even if your sales pitch is great!)

Description: This incredible new machine is capable of producing music with a simple turn of the crank. Various cylinders are loaded onto a turning mechanism that mixes various noises into music. The pleasant sound is then amplified through the tube in the front, using no electricity at all.

Factors of Production:
Materials: $22.48
Labor: $21.65
Packaging: $8.45
Total: $52.58
Note: Additional cylinders cost $24.95.

Tomorrow, you will deliver a 1-minute sales pitch for this product. Be as convincing and persuasive as possible, because your goal is to make everyone in the room want to go out and buy this product. Remember to include a name for the product, a brief description of it, an explanation of its purpose, and how much it costs.

SALES PITCH PRESENTATION RUBRIC

	MASTER SALESPERSON	SALESPERSON EXTRAORDINAIRE	SALESPERSON IN TRAINING
EYE CONTACT	The salesperson maintains eye contact with the audience at all times.	The salesperson looks up from time to time and makes eye contact.	The salesperson reads from a paper, looking up only once or twice.
PROJECTION	The salesperson can easily be heard by everyone in the room.	The salesperson can be heard by most of the people in the room.	The salesperson can be heard by only the people in the front of the room.
ENUNCIATION	The salesperson can be clearly understood throughout the speech.	The salesperson can be clearly understood some of the time.	It is difficult to understand the salesperson.
TEMPO	The sales pitch is given at a pace which helps maintain audience interest.	The sales pitch is either too slow or too fast, but the audience pays attention.	The sales pitch is so slow or so fast that the audience is bored or confused.
ORGANIZATION	The sales pitch has an easy-to-follow pattern, making it easy for the audience to understand the information being delivered.	The sales pitch follows a pattern, but the transitions from one topic to another are abrupt.	The sales pitch jumps from subject to subject with no discernable pattern.

EARNINGS STATEMENT

	DATE	REASON	AMOUNT	TOTAL
1				
2				
3				
4				
5				
6				
7				
8				
9				
10				

Lesson 2

Concepts

- Government's impact on the economy
- Banks' impact on the economy
- Consumers' roles in the economy

Materials

- PowerPoint presentation (*Welcome to Ecopolis*; available at http://www. prufrock.com/client/downloads/ecopolis.cfm; PDF version also available)
- Facts of Ecopolis sheet (p. 36)
- Ecopolitan Responsibilities sheet (p. 38)
- Role Distribution sheet (p. 40)
- Journal entry form (p. 41)
- Menu of issues for campaign speeches (p. 42)
- Folders for students' paperwork

Student Objective

Students become familiar with the nature of Ecopolis and with the various roles and assorted responsibilities.

Introduction

Students view *Welcome to Ecopolis*, a PowerPoint presentation describing Ecopolis. (If you elect not to show the PowerPoint, you can describe its contents in a different way, such as with an outline on the board.) Students should be familiarized with the system of priority seating and with the salaries earned by elected officials (the Head Honcho gets $5,000; the Big Deal gets $3,000; Deep Pockets gets $2,000; and Money Bags each get $1,000).

Recognition

Through class discussion, students identify the roles in Ecopolis and the object of the game, asking questions to clarify anything they do not understand. Students also write daily journal entries detailing their experiences in the unit. From this point forward, students are to write a journal entry for every day of the unit.

Application

Students are assigned roles (some preliminary) for the simulation.
1. Bankers are appointed based on the results of the Banker Selection Qualifier.
2. The remaining students are assigned temporary roles as either candidates or campaign managers.
3. After a discussion of how Ecopolis works, candidates, campaign managers, and bankers react to their role assignments by writing about what they wish to accomplish in their journals.

Problem Solving

Students develop strategies to enable success (i.e., maximize the holding of assets) in Ecopolis.

Grade-Level Expectations

The student:
*   Identifies the role of the individual in factor and product markets.
*   Recognizes the relationships between productivity and wages, and between wages and standards of living.
*   Recognizes that shortages and surpluses affect the price and availability of goods and services.

Additional Notes

*   Define the roles of bankers, politicians, and citizens for students. The interactions among these groups drive the unit, so all students must understand the roles and their associated responsibilities.
*   Discuss with students the connection between hard work (effort) and success (a good grade). Students should consider the opportunity cost of each decision they make.
*   Use the Banker Selection Qualifier to help you decide which students will become bankers. There are four bankers, two for each bank. You may tell students that each bank should have an accounts manager and a loan officer, and allow them to work out for themselves how to divide up the work. This

will help them understand the importance of specialization and division of labor.

- Use students' sales pitch presentations to decide who may be good candidates for public office. Remaining students (not bankers or candidates) serve, temporarily, as campaign managers. Students selected as candidates need to be able to lead their peers and to express themselves well as public speakers. They do not necessarily have to be the best students. There are three candidates for each role (Head Honcho, Big Deal, and Deep Pockets), totaling nine candidates, and each candidate can have a campaign manager. After familiarizing yourself with this unit, you will have a good idea of which students would make the best candidates. Students will not have a thorough understanding of the responsibilities elected officials will have prior to being elected, but rather, they will learn how to handle these responsibilities as the unit progresses.

- Each of the nine candidates can have a campaign manager. Campaign managers are destined to become Ecopolitan consumers. As campaign managers, they learn about economic issues, thus becoming more informed voters. Encourage campaign managers to be actively involved in their candidates' campaigns. Inform campaign managers that those whose candidates win will be rewarded with bonuses equal to 10% of the candidates' respective salaries, meaning that three of the campaign managers stand to profit considerably from a win. (This is a one-time bonus; these three campaign managers will not be paid again along with the politicians in Lesson 7.) Please note that it is up to your discretion how to divide up students if you have a smaller or larger group. You may decide to create an additional bank, assistant positions, and so on.

- We have provided a menu of issues for the campaign speeches on page 42. You can distribute these to students at the end of this lesson, so that they can begin to think about their speeches outside of class, or you can wait until the beginning of Lesson 3 and then give political candidates and their campaign managers more guidance in terms of their campaign issues.

- Each student should write a daily journal entry detailing his or her experiences in Ecopolis. This can be done at the beginning of class, at the end of class, or as a homework assignment, and it is up to you whether you want to check these journal entries regularly. The provided journal entry form is fairly nonspecific, as students should be encouraged to reflect on whatever aspects of the simulation most interest them. If students request guidelines for what to write about, however, you might use prompting questions including the following:
  o   What happened today? How did it make you feel?

o What does it feel like to be a politican/banker/Ecopolitan? What do students playing other roles not understand about your role?

o What are some of the problems you have faced in your pursuit of preferred seating?

o What suggestions do you have for improving Ecopolis?

o What could you do to help yourself be more successful?

o What could you do to help others be more successful?

- Use your creativity to develop attractive preferred seating. This could entail using luxury chairs or utilizing the classic real estate mantra: location, location, location! Some teachers have used armchairs, rolling desk chairs, and even plush sofas, whereas others have made preferred seating involve privileges such as a complimentary daily snack or proximity to the window.

- To illustrate the concept of scarcity, the seats should be priced according to a specific scheme. The first seat sold should be priced at $10,000, whereas each subsequent seat should cost $2,000 more than the previous seat sold. We suggest that you make a total of five seats available in order to demonstrate the concept of scarcity. Therefore, you would have seats costing $10,000; $12,000; $14,000; $16,000; and $18,000. These seats are all available from the beginning of the simulation, and they should be purchased on a first-come, first-served basis. Typically, the 20% down payment required (along with the set amount of loan money available from the banks) limits the number of students who can buy preferred seating, and many students lose their seats when they are unable to repay their loans. Once students get the hang of the simulation, however, they are likely to become creative—we have had students rent out their seats for profit. Later on, likely before all of the seats have been purchased, the economy will be challenged. This will stem from the fact that as each seat is purchased, the money used to buy that seat exits Ecopolis when it is paid to the Ecomaster (teacher). This will illustrate the concept of global interdependence. (Students will not realize that this is happening until later on in the unit.)

- Let's take a few minutes to discuss the flow of money in Ecopolis. As the Ecomaster, you have the power to generate money simply by making an entry on students' earning reports. For example, a student can earn $500 by getting an A on a test simply because you added that amount to his account. Similarly, on the day that the political candidates are elected to office (in Lesson 5), you will credit the Head Honcho's account with $5,000, the Big Deal's account with $3,000, and Deep Pockets's account with $2,000. When bankers begin working on their tutorial, reward each of them with $1,000. (We like to make a show of this, giving incentives to the other students to find ways to earn money.) Additionally, each bank will be given $10,000 to start with. The government will also be given $10,000 to start with. They must use this money to offer $500 stipends to Ecopolitans who have not earned $1,000 total during preparations for the simulation.

From this point forward, however, the Ecomaster (who represents the global economy) does not simply give money to Ecopolis. The Ecomaster pays the banks interest on whatever money they have in accounts overnight (4%), and the banks also receive loan repayments from customers at a 5% interest. Banks give their customers 2% interest on their accounts, so they are paid with the bank's profits. The Ecomaster collects the money from preferred seating sales. The government receives tax money from Ecopolitans, who continue to make money, and they must figure out who will pay them. (Depending on the goods and services they provide, this could be the government, individuals, or the Ecomaster.) They must also continue to make tax payments as they earn money. The elected officials are paid for the second time in Lesson 7, and their salaries come out of tax money. In Lesson 7, $500 stipends are again given to those Ecopolitans who still have not earned $1,000 (this money is furnished by tax dollars as well).

You may wish to make your own PowerPoint presentation or develop a poster to help students keep track of the events of Ecopolis. We also suggest that you either provide students with folders or have them bring in their own, in order to keep track of the considerable amount of paperwork involved in the simulation. At this stage, try to ensure that students understand enough to begin the simulation, but also try to allow them to figure out as much as possible on their own. This balance is difficult to strike, but allowing students to discover the nuances of their economy will help them to better internalize the concepts—and have more fun!

FACTS OF ECOPOLIS

People of Ecopolis

- **Head Honcho:** The leader has great responsibility and great privileges. He or she receives a $5,000 salary after being elected.
- **Big Deal:** The assistant leader supports the Head Honcho while advocating for the Ecopolitans. The Big Deal receives a salary of $3,000 after being elected.
- **Deep Pockets:** The treasury chairman regulates the money supply of Ecopolis. He or she must collect taxes, keep the government accounts in order, and oversee banking policies. Deep Pockets receives a $2,000 salary upon being elected.
- **Money Bags:** Bankers keep customers' accounts straight and manage loans for their clients. Their initial salaries are $1,000. Bankers qualify for their positions by performing well on the Banker Selection Qualifier.
- **John Q. and Jane Q. Public:** These citizens make up the engine of Ecopolis. They must find a way to make money, protect it in their bank accounts, and achieve the Ecopolitan dream.

Key Point

All Ecopolitans, from the Head Honcho to the consumers, have the same dream . . . to own a little piece of heaven in preferred seating!

Where Does the Money Come From?

- Ecopolitans earn money through homework, community service, and other good behavior prior to the start of the unit, and they can continue to earn money throughout the unit.
- Each student opens a savings account that earns daily interest.
- Elected officials are paid salaries by the government.
- Bankers collect a salary from the bank's profits.

Everyone Pays Taxes!

- Citizens of Ecopolis elect government officials.
- Government officials determine the fiscal (money) requirements of Ecopolis.
- These required amounts are paid by Ecopolitans through taxes.
- Everyone pays a percentage of his or her earnings to the government.
- The government provides the promised services to all Ecopolitans.

The Ecopolitans are the engine of Ecopolis. All of the Ecopolitans (the Head Honcho, the Big Deal, Deep Pockets, Money Bags, and John Q. and Jane Q. Public) are eligible to buy a seat in preferred seating if they can afford it!

ECOPOLITAN RESPONSIBILITIES

1. What is your role?

    _____

    _____

    _____

    _____

    _____

    _____

    _____

2. What are your responsibilities?

    _____

    _____

    _____

    _____

    _____

    _____

    _____

    _____

3. What is the issue you must deal with?

    _____

    _____

    _____

    _____

    _____

Name:_____ Date: _____

Plan for Role Success

Tomorrow, I plan to . . .

_____

_____

_____

_____

_____

_____

I plan to do this because . . .

_____

_____

_____

_____

_____

_____

_____

ROLE DISTRIBUTION

After all students take the Banker Selection Qualifier (BSQ), all students prepare sales pitches to demonstrate their public-speaking skills.

The top four scorers on the BSQ become the Money Bags (bankers).

The top nine sales-pitch performers become the candidates.

The remaining students are campaign managers and are assigned to candidates.

BANKERS complete the bankers' tutorial.

CANDIDATES FOR HEAD HONCHO (the leader) and their **campaign managers** research and write speeches about resource allocation.

CANDIDATES FOR BIG DEAL (the assistant leader) and their **campaign managers** work on speeches about wants vs. needs.

CANDIDATES FOR DEEP POCKETS (the treasury chairperson) and their **campaign managers** work on speeches about costs and taxes.

JOHN Q. AND JANE Q. PUBLIC
ALL STUDENTS LISTEN TO THE CANDIDATES' SPEECHES AND VOTE IN THE ELECTION!

Name:_____ Date: _____

JOURNAL ENTRY

Each day during your experience in Ecopolis, you must record your experiences and reflections in the form of a journal entry. At the end of the unit, you will be responsible for producing a complete set of journal entries as part of a final project.

Daily Activities

My beginning balance today was _____

I earned _____ today by doing the following:

_____

Tomorrow, I plan to accomplish the following in terms of finances:

_____

_____

_____

Reflections and Expectations

I wish I had . . .

_____

_____

_____

_____

_____

Tomorrow, I plan to do the following:

_____

_____

_____

_____

_____

Ecopolis © Prufrock Press Inc.   41

Permission is granted to photocopy or reproduce this page for single classroom use only.

MENU OF ISSUES FOR CAMPAIGN SPEECHES

Head Honcho (Resource Allocation)

1. What are the qualities of a good leader? How will those qualities help you govern Ecopolis?
2. As the leader of Ecopolis, how will you manage its resources? How do the concepts of supply and demand come into play? How are you going to handle scarcity?
3. Is it a misallocation of resources for an Ecopolitan to choose not to do his or her homework when money is available for compensation? Should the government bail this person out when he or she does not have enough money? How will you help the Ecopolitans use their resources wisely?

Big Deal (Wants vs. Needs)

1. Describe the differences between needs and wants. How will you encourage Ecopolitans to differentiate between needs and wants in Ecopolis?
2. Part of your job description, if you are elected, will be to help the Ecopolitans achieve their economic dreams. How will you encourage them to earn enough money? Provide concrete, step-by-step examples that Ecopolitans can follow to achieve success.

Deep Pockets (Taxes and Costs)

1. Explain the concept of opportunity costs and how opportunity costs affect the choices that Ecopolitans need to make.
2. How will you justify the need for taxes to Ecopolitans? How might Ecopolitans see their taxes at work?

Lesson 3

Concepts

- Resource allocation
- Wants vs. needs
- Taxes and costs

Materials

- Money Bags (Banker) Job Description sheet (p. 46)
- Banker tutorial (pp. 47–62)
- Resource lesson (pp. 63–66)
- Helpful Hints sheet (p. 67)
- Menu of issues for campaign speeches (p. 42)

Student Objectives

Students playing the role of banker should demonstrate an understanding of the bank's role in a free market economy. Students playing candidate and campaign manager roles should research and explore various economic issues that may affect Ecopolis.

Introduction

Divide students into four groups: bankers, leader candidates and campaign managers, assistant leader candidates and campaign managers, and treasury chairperson candidates and campaign managers. Review the various roles with students. Give bankers a copy of their job description and the 2-day banker tutorial. Give candidates and campaign managers the menu of issues for campaign speeches, if you have not yet done so, and the Helpful Hints sheet (unless you opt not to wait until later on to provide this).

Recognition

Each group describes its role to the other groups.

Application

Students split up to begin understanding their roles and the various issues associated with their roles.

1. Bankers begin work on the banker tutorial.
2. Candidates and their campaign managers are assigned issues. All candidates for a given position must speak on the same issue so that voters can compare them objectively. (The provided materials assume that Head Honcho candidates will speak on the topic of resource allocation, Big Deal candidates will speak on the topic of wants vs. needs, and Deep Pockets candidates will speak on the topic of taxation in a market economy.)
3. Candidates and campaign managers must explore these issues, discuss them amongst themselves, and research them using whatever resources they can in order to gain a better understanding of the topics and deliver the best speeches possible. (They might use the Internet, interview the teacher or other adults, go to the library, and so on.)

Problem Solving

Students discuss their various roles in terms of how they will affect other students and the unit overall.

1. Bankers discuss the vital role the bank will play in Ecopolis.
2. Candidates and campaign managers discuss how the issues they are assigned will affect life in Ecopolis.

Grade-Level Expectations

The student:

- Recognizes the relationships between productivity and wages and between wages and standards of living.
- Determines the opportunity cost of decisions.
- Recognizes that shortage and surplus affect the price and availability of goods and services.

Additional Notes

- During the first day of this lesson, bankers will begin working on the banker tutorial. We suggest that you allow them to work in a private space, such as in an adjoining classroom, in the school's media center, or in the hallway outside of your classroom. In this tutorial, bankers work through a series of example problems and then learn to use all of the bank forms that they will be in charge of in Ecopolis. You will also want to familiarize yourself with these forms so that you can make sure that students are completing them correctly. These forms include the Ecopolis Savings Account sheet (p. 56), the Bank Daily Summary sheet (p. 58), and the Loan Calculation sheet (p. 62).

- Because there is much to do (particularly if your students struggle with time management), you might consider setting interim goals to ensure that students are able to complete all of their assigned work in 2 days. Specifically, you might instruct bankers to try to reach Example 4 (the Bank Daily Summary sheet) by the end of the first day, and you might recommend to candidates and campaign managers that they complete their research and discussions by the end of the first day, so that they can have adequate time to compose and rehearse their speeches. If you anticipate that negative campaigning could be an issue, you might set some guidelines for your students.

- The banker tutorial is designed so that students direct their own learning; do not be surprised, however, if they approach you frequently with questions. It is our experience that the tutorial works best when a teacher is available to help students, particularly as students often crave reassurance that they are doing the work correctly. In our experience, bankers need the entire allotted time to spend on the tutorial.

- Candidates and their campaign managers will be introduced to the issues on which speeches will be prepared: The Head Honcho candidates' topic is resource allocation, the Big Deal candidates will discuss wants vs. needs, and Deep Pockets candidates will speak to taxation in a market economy. With these speeches, candidates will teach the rest of the class about these issues. It is up to you whether or not to comment on their speeches or augment them with additional information.

- Only the most astute students will question the role of foreign nations in Ecopolis. They will not realize that as the teacher (Ecomaster), you represent foreign countries. Every time somebody pays for preferred seating, money leaves the country, because preferred seats are not made by Ecopolitans—they are imported. (This will be explained further in Lesson 7.) In the eyes of most students, preferred seating simply appears. Students must learn that someone must provide the resources necessary for the seats' construction. For example, let us say that a student purchases the first preferred seat. He provides a 20% down payment ($2,000), and a bank loans him the remaining $8,000. This money is collected by the teacher, who deducts $2,000 from the student's account and $8,000 from the bank's account. Students generally do not question this until presented with the second issue of *The Rug Tug Times* explaining the problem. In this way, the unit is designed to address global interdependence.

- Remind students that there are only five preferred seats available for sale (unless they find a way to create additional seats) in order to underscore the issue of scarcity. Inform students that preferred seats become progressively more expensive ($10,000; $12,000; $14,000; $16,000; and $18,000) due to the impact that reduced supply has on price.

MONEY BAGS (BANKER)
JOB DESCRIPTION

Congratulations! Due to your outstanding performance on the Banker Selection Qualifier, you have been chosen to serve as Money Bags (a banker) in Ecopolis during this unit. You have passed the Banker Selection Qualifier with flying colors, and you are being awarded a $1,000 bonus that you may add to your earnings sheet. Later on, you will make money from the bank's profits. This will be explained further in your training materials.

As Money Bags, you have the responsibility of adding enough liquidity (money in circulation) to give citizens of Ecopolis the opportunity to buy preferred seating. It will also be necessary for the bank to service savings accounts for its customers.

To accomplish these goals, you and your partner should split your responsibilities, playing two distinct roles. One of you will be a **customer service manager**, and one of you will be a **loan officer**. You can determine for yourselves how best to divide up tasks and responsibilities.

You and your partner will have to help one another in order to succeed in Ecopolis, but do not forget that each of you has a primary responsibility. Your success depends on the success of your clients—John Q. and Jane Q. Public, the consumers. You must also decide whether or not you will buy a preferred seat for yourself.

Don't forget that you will have the Head Honcho (the leader of Ecopolis), the Big Deal (the assistant leader), and Deep Pockets (the tax collector and treasury chairperson) to rely on for guidance. Now it is time to begin the tutorial that will enable you to perform your role, which is vital to everyone's success in Ecopolis.

Good luck! You are going to earn every penny of your $1,000 salary.

Banker:_____

Partner:_____ Date: _____

BANKER TUTORIAL

Dear Banker,

You will spend two class periods preparing for the opening of business while your classmates work on filling the remaining roles that are needed for Ecopolis to operate smoothly. You and your partner will work together on this tutorial, which will guide you toward success in your new roles. Although you will need to work independently, you can ask for help from the teacher if you are struggling.

In general, the idea is for your bank to make money by satisfying human (Ecopolitan) needs and wants. As Ecopolis begins, there are two ways in which your bank can earn profits. First, you can get Ecopolitans—including yourselves and politicians—to open up savings accounts. Second, you can help satisfy the wants of your fellow citizens by offering them loans so that they can purchase preferred seating. There are other ways you can earn profits, but you will have to figure them out as you go along!

In the money business, savings account deposits flow into the bank, and loan money flows out.

You'll need to know some vocabulary first. It's important that you understand what *principal*, *rate*, *interest*, and *term* mean.

- **Principal:** the amount of money saved or borrowed
- **Rate:** the percentage the bank pays or charges its customers
- **Interest:** the amount of money the bank pays or charges its customers, or the amount of money the bank makes from the government
- **Term:** the length of time for which money is borrowed

There is a formula that brings all of these terms together so that you can do calculations.

$$I = P \times R \times T$$
$$I = \text{interest}$$
$$P = \text{principal}$$
$$R = \text{rate}$$
$$T = \text{term}$$

In real life, T—the term—measures time in years. In this unit, however, the term will be measured in days. In other words, a T value of 1 means 1 day, instead of 1 year.

Now let's begin learning how banks make money. Money will flow into your bank when Ecopolitans open savings accounts by making deposits. To encourage citizens to deposit money into your bank, you will pay interest to your customers at the rate of 2% on any amount they leave in the bank overnight.

Let's consider the formula I = P x R x T again to see how it can be used to satisfy your customers' need to make money.

EXAMPLE 1: Linda opens a savings account on a Tuesday by depositing $1,500 in your bank. To determine how much money she will have in the bank on Wednesday, let us use the formula I = P x R x T.

$$I = P \times R \times T$$
$$P = \$1,500$$
$$R = .02$$
$$T = 1$$
$$1,500 \times .02 \times 1 = 30$$

The amount of the deposit is called the principal, in this case $1,500. The percentage that your bank paid her is the rate, in this case 2%. The amount of time Linda's money is in the bank is called the term, in this case 1 day. The amount of money the bank pays to Linda is the interest, in this case $30.

By multiplying principal by rate by time, we get interest. Therefore, the next day (Wednesday), when Linda comes into the Ecopolis bank, she finds that she has $1,530 in her savings account. This is the original principal of $1,500 plus the interest, $30.

Name:_____ Date: _____

EXAMPLE 2: Frank deposits $475 overnight. How much money does he have the next day?

$$I = P \times R \times T$$
$$P = \$475$$
$$R = 2\%$$
$$T = 1 \text{ day}$$
$$475 \times .02 \times 1 = 9.50$$

Using the formula, you can see that when Frank returns to your bank the next day, he finds that he has $484.50 in his account—the principal amount of $475 plus the interest of $9.50.

Try the following exercises individually, and then see whether your partner got the same answer that you did. Answers are provided after the examples, but don't look ahead!

EXERCISE 1: A customer deposits $1,725 on Tuesday. What is the new balance on Wednesday?

EXERCISE 2: A customer deposits $1,200 on Monday. What is the new balance on Wednesday?

Check to see whether your answers are correct.
- **Exercise 1:** $1,759.50
- **Exercise 2:** $1,248.48 (Don't forget that because the term is 2 days, you must calculate the interest earned for the first night, and then use that total amount to calculate the interest earned for the second night.)

If you and your banking partner got these two problems correct, then you should move on. If your partner is confused, try to explain to him or her how to do the problem(s). If both you and your partner are confused, then try the practice problems in the Resource Lesson sheet and the sheets labeled Activity A and Activity B at the back of this tutorial.

It will be necessary for you to keep track of your customers' savings accounts. You must also ensure that your customers know how to fill out copies to keep for their own records, because they will not have completed this tutorial.

Banking Forms

In this packet, there are two forms called Example Ecopolis Savings Account (pp. 56–57). Pull these out and look at them frequently as you are reading. You will notice that one of these is to be kept by the banker (the banker copy), and one is to be kept by the customer (the customer copy).

You must ensure that the banker copy stays with the bank at all times. Also, these two copies must match up exactly. Always remember to put the date on these forms so that you can have a record of what happened on a given day.

You must be able to complete this form for your bank, and you must also be able to teach your customers how to maintain these forms for their own portfolios. Here are descriptions of each part of the Ecopolis Savings Account form:

Column A (BALANCE): This is the amount of money customers have in the bank at the beginning of each day. It **must match up** with Column E from the prior day, which shows the customer's final balance (amount of money) from the day before. In other words, the amount of money that a customer has in the bank at the end of business on Tuesday must be equal to the amount that he or she has at the beginning of the day on Wednesday.

Column B (DEPOSITS): This is where you will enter any deposits that customers bring to your bank.

Column C (WITHDRAWALS): If a client takes money out of the bank (for example, if he or she needs money to buy preferred seating), then this column is where you would write down the amount of money that he or she took out.

Column D (INTEREST): This is the column you will use to determine how much money a customer has in the bank at the end of the day and overnight (the final balance). You will need this number to figure out how much interest the customer is paid according to the amount that he or she has in the account.

Let's work through the example shown on the Ecopolis Savings Account sheets. Look at the banker copy.

Peggy begins with a balance of $0 (this is shown in Column A). Peggy deposits $3,000 from her Earnings Statement into her savings account (this is shown in Column B). Be sure she has paid her taxes before coming to your bank! Because she runs out of time, she does not withdraw any of her money. Therefore, there is a "0" entered in Column C. Peggy is going to leave $3,000 in your bank overnight. She will earn interest on this amount, which you must calculate and enter in Column D.

To calculate the amount of interest to enter in Column D, use the formula $I = P \times R \times T$.

Because T is 1, we will not show it. The principal amount is the initial amount (Column A) plus the money that came into the account or left the account that day, meaning any deposits that were made (Column B) minus any withdrawals that were made (Column C). The new formula becomes $.02 (A + (B - C)) = D$, the interest paid on the account.

Formula: $.02 (A + (B - C)) = D$
Substitute: $.02 (0 + (\$3{,}000 - 0)) = D$
Solve: $D = 60$

So Peggy earned $60 of interest on her account. This means that Peggy's final balance is $3,060—if you look, you'll see that the banker copy and the customer copy both show this. It is very important that these forms match up exactly!

Try the following exercise on your own, and then check the sheet labeled Practice Ecopolis Savings Account Form (p. 58) to see if you and your partner are on track.

EXERCISE 3: Peggy comes back to your bank on Day 2. She deposits an additional $14,500 and also withdraws $4,000 to meet some of her expenses. Calculate what her balance will be at the beginning of Day 3.

Check the practice sheet to see whether you are correct. If you and your partner are both confused, speak with your teacher. If not, it is time to learn how *you* get to make money!

Bank Earnings

You are paying customers 2% on the amounts they have deposited in your bank overnight. However, the Ecopolis Federal Reserve System ("The Fed") pays your bank 4% on the amount of money in your bank overnight.

In addition, your bank will be opening with an initial balance of $10,000 in addition to the money deposited by investors. The way interest is calculated for your bank is the same way that interest is calculated for your customers. The difference is that you get 4%, whereas your customers get 2%.

The Bank Daily Summary form must be filled out at the end of each day. It is a record showing how much money your bank will make by keeping money overnight.

Let's go through the example shown on the sheet labeled Example Bank Daily Summary (p. 60).

This example shows a beginning balance of $10,000 (Column A). A total of six customers came to your bank to deposit a total of $15,500 (Column B) and made total withdrawals of $3,000 (Column C). Note carefully that the amount in Column B ($15,500) was calculated by adding up all of the deposits made by your customers. To do this, you will add all of the amounts in Column B of the Ecopolis Savings Account sheets. The amount in Column C ($3,000) was calculated by finding the total amount withdrawn by all of your customers.

To calculate the amount of interest your bank will earn overnight from the federal government, use the formula shown in Column D of the Bank Daily Summary.

Formula: $(A + (B - C)) \times .04 = D$
Substitute: $(\$10,000 + (\$15,500 - \$3,000)) \times .04 = D$
Solve: $(\$10,000 + \$12,500) \times .04 = D$
$(\$22,500) \times .04 = D$
$\$900 = D$

So in this example, the federal government pays you $900 to have your money in this account overnight. Column E shows the amount you paid in interest to all of your customers. Remember that in Exercise 3, you paid Peggy $271.20 in interest. Column E will show that amount added to all of the other interest amounts you had to pay to customers (this column shows the total amount of money the bank paid customers in interest). To calculate the bank's final balance at the end of the day, you will use the formula shown in Column F.

$$A + B + D - C - E = F$$
$$\$10,000 + \$15,500 - \$3,000 + \$900 - \$271.20 = F$$
$$\$23,128.80 = F$$

Notice that the balance in Column A on any given day should be the same as the final balance from the day before.

Try the following exercise, and then see if you are correct by checking the sheet labeled Practice Bank Daily Summary (p. 61).

EXERCISE 4: Let us say that on Day 2, four customers came to your bank to deposit a total of $8,500. Additionally, two other customers withdrew a total of $1,000. Let us say that you paid out a total of $775 in interest to your customers. Determine your starting balance for Day 3.

Make sure that you are correct! Now you have learned about one way that the bank can make money: by taking in as much money as possible from Ecopolitans and keeping it overnight so that you earn 4% interest on their accounts.

There is another way for you to make even more money for your bank. If Ecopolitans are to buy preferred seating, then they will likely need a loan—just as adults need loans to make large purchases, like for a house or a car. Very few people have enough cash to make such large purchases without the help of a bank. The same is true in Ecopolis. Preferred seats in Ecopolis are expensive—the lowest priced seat costs $10,000. Ecopolitans have earned some money, paid their taxes, and opened savings accounts at your bank. Very few of them, if any, have enough cash left over to buy a preferred seat. Here is where the bank can earn additional income by helping customers satisfy one of their wants. To make loans, you may loan money to your customers at an interest rate of 5%, meaning that they will have to repay you not only the money they borrow, but also 5% of the amount that they borrow.

The following explanation will help you learn how to figure out the amount of the daily payment (interest) customers will owe you once you have loaned them money with which to buy preferred seating. Remember that to calculate savings account interest, I = P x R x T.

- Step 1: A customer comes to you wanting to purchase a preferred seat.
- Step 2: The bank requires a 20% down payment to protect the bank's investment. This means that whatever the cost of the preferred seating is, the customer needs to pay the bank 20% of that amount. The bank pays the remainder of the cost.
- Step 3: The bank loans the customer the amount he or she needs in order to complete the purchase.
- Step 4: The bank pays Deep Pockets a $100 fee. That's right—Deep Pockets gets $100 every time the bank makes a loan!
- Step 5: The bank collects 5% of the principal each day.

It can get rather complicated, so let's do an example to help you understand. Look at the Example Loan Calculation form (p. 62) now. Alice has $3,000 in her savings account, and she wants to purchase a seat that costs $12,000 (see Column A). The down payment, then, is $12,000 x .20 = $2,400 (see Column B). The amount of the loan will be the cost of the seat minus the down payment. In this case, that is $12,000 – $2,400 = $9,600 (see Column C). Next, the bank pays Deep Pockets a $100 fee. Then, use the formula I = P x R x T to calculate the amount of interest that Alice must pay the bank for each day that she owns the seat and has money left to pay off: I = $9,600 x .05 x 1 = $480. Finally, the total of $12,000 ($9,600 from the bank, and $2,400 from Alice) is turned over to the Ecomaster to pay for the preferred seating.

This diagram shows the problem we just went through in a form you might understand better.

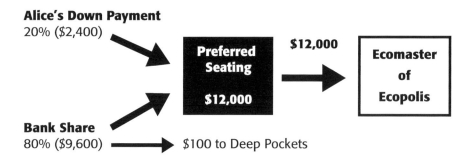

Try the following two exercises to see if you get the correct answers. You'll find the answers after the exercises, but do not look ahead!

EXERCISE 5: Let's say that a preferred seat costs $16,000. Determine the amount of down payment needed from the customer, the bank's share of the purchase price (that is, the amount the bank will have to pay), and the daily payment due to the bank from the customer.

EXERCISE 6: Let's say that a preferred seat costs $20,000. Determine the amount of down payment needed from the customer, the bank's share of the purchase price (that is, the amount the bank will have to pay), and the daily payment due to the bank from the customer.

> **ALERT!** If a customer is unwilling or unable to make his or her daily payment to the bank, inform the Big Deal immediately that the preferred seat is in *foreclosure*. You will be given forms later on to deal with this situation.

Remember the 20% down payment that had to be made to protect your bank? Here's how that works. If the customer is unable to make a payment, the bank *forecloses* on the property. This means that the bank takes the property, in this case the preferred seat, from the customer and may sell it to the highest bidder. The following is an example of how this unfortunate situation is fixed.

- Alice bought a seat that had a price of $12,000.
- Alice made her first daily payment of $480. (If she were responsible, she would have paid off some of the principal amount—the sooner it is paid off, the sooner she stops having to pay interest!)
- Alice could not make her second daily payment, because she did not finish her homework, so she did not receive her usual payment.
- The bank informs the Big Deal immediately.
- Alice loses, or *forfeits*, her down payment of $2,400. (This is very sad for her, but the bank has to protect its own business.)
- The bank now owns the preferred seat and can auction it off to the highest bidder. As long as somebody pays at least $9,600 for the seat, then the bank will not have lost money—because if you recall, that is the amount that the bank originally contributed for the purchase of the seat.

To summarize, you—as a banker—can make a profit by opening and maintaining savings accounts for your customers, as well as making loans so that your customers can buy preferred seating. You can earn income while providing a service to Ecopolitans that satisfies their needs and wants. Your customers are getting interest payments, and so are you. Dollars are flowing smoothly in Ecopolis, and it is your job to make this good fortune continue. Hopefully, you have learned your lessons well—Ecopolitans are depending on you!

Answers to Exercises:

5. A = $3,200; B = $12,800; C = $640 per day
6. A = $4,000; B = $16,000; C = $800 per day

Banker: _____

Customer: _____ Date: _____

EXAMPLE ECOPOLIS SAVINGS ACCOUNT FORM (Banker Copy)

Day	A Balance	B Deposits	C Withdrawals	D Interest (2%) .02 x (A + (B – C))	E Final balance A + B + D – C
1	0	$3,000	0	$3,000 x .02 = $60	$3,060
2	$3,060				
3					
4					
Totals					

Ecopolis © Prufrock Press Inc.

Customer: _____

Banker: _____ Date: _____

EXAMPLE ECOPOLIS SAVINGS ACCOUNT FORM (Customer Copy)

Day	A Balance	B Deposits	C Withdrawals	D Interest (2%) .02 x (A + (B – C))	E Final balance A + B + D – C
1	0	$3,000	0	$3,000 x .02 = $60	$3,060
2	$3,060				
3					
4					
Totals					

Banker: _____

Customer: _____ Date: _____

PRACTICE ECOPOLIS SAVINGS ACCOUNT FORM
(Banker Copy)

Day	A Balance	B Deposits	C Withdrawals	D Interest (2%) .02 x (A + (B − C))	E Final balance A + B + D − C
1	0	$3,000	0	$3,000 x .02 = $60	$3,060
2	$3,060	$14,500	$4,000	(.02)($13,560) = $271.20	$13,831.20
3	$13,831.20				
4					
Totals					

Customer: _____

Banker: _____ Date: _____

PRACTICE ECOPOLIS SAVINGS ACCOUNT FORM
(Customer Copy)

Day	A Balance	B Deposits	C Withdrawals	D Interest (2%) .02 x (A + (B − C))	E Final balance A + B + D − C
1	0	$3,000	0	$3,000 x .02 = $60	$3,060
2	$3,060	$14,500	$4,000	(.02)($13,560) = $271.20	$13,831.20
3	$13,831.20				
4					
Totals					

Banker: _____ Date: _____

EXAMPLE BANK DAILY SUMMARY

Transaction	A Balance	B Total deposits (from Ecopolis Savings Accounts)	C Total withdrawals (from Ecopolis Savings Accounts)	D Bank earnings (4%) (A + (B – C)) x .04 =	E Total interest expenses (from Ecopolis Savings Accounts Column D)	F Final balance A + B + D – C – E =
1	$10,000	$15,500 (total from six customers)	$3,000	$900	$271.20	$23,128.80
2	$23,128.80					
3						
4						
Totals						

Banker: _____ Date: _____

PRACTICE BANK DAILY SUMMARY

Transaction	A Balance	B Total deposits (from Ecopolis Savings Accounts)	C Total withdrawals (from Ecopolis Savings Accounts)	D Bank earnings (4%) $(A + (B - C)) \times .04 =$	E Total interest expenses (from Ecopolis Savings Accounts Column D)	F Final balance $A + B + D - C - E =$
1	$10,000	$15,500 (total from six customers)	$3,000	$900	$271.20	$23,128.80
2	$23,128.80	$8,500	$1,000	$1,225.15	$775	$31,078.95
3	$31,078.95					
4						
Totals						

Banker:_____

Customer:_____ Date:_____

EXAMPLE LOAN CALCULATION FORM

Day	A Total price of seat	B Down payment required A x .20 = B	C Amount of loan A − B = C	D Daily interest due (5%) C x .05 = D	Date paid	Date paid	Date paid	Date paid	Date paid	Date paid
1	$12,000	$12,000 x .20 = $2,400	$9,600	$9,600 x .05 = $480						
2										
3										
4										
Totals										

Ecopolis © Prufrock Press Inc.
Permission is granted to photocopy or reproduce this page for single classroom use only.

RESOURCE LESSON

The following lesson will help you understand decision variables and how to solve percent problems. You'll need to watch out for the word "of"!

When the word "of" <u>connects</u> two numbers, you will want to <u>multiply</u>.

Multiplication is commutative, which means that you can multiply the same set of numbers in any order and still get the same result. Therefore, it doesn't matter which number is the *multiplicand* (number to be multiplied) or which is the *multiplier* (number of times it is multiplied). Reminder: multiplicand x multiplier = product.

$$a \times b = b \times a$$

Example: _____ is 80% of 90. (Remember that to use percentages in equations, you should convert them to decimals. 80% is represented as .8.)

.8 x 90 = 72

When the word "of" <u>does not connect</u> two numbers, you will want to <u>divide</u>.

Division is not commutative. Order matters when you are dividing! The dividend (the numerator of the fraction, or what is being divided) and the divisor (the denominator of the fraction, or the number of times the dividend is being divided) must be in the correct places.

$$a \div b \neq b \div a$$

The first hint that may help you is that when the word "of" does not connect two numbers, and when the percentage is available, you should divide by the percentage.

Example: 9% of _____ is 36.

36 ÷ .09 = 400

If you cannot use the first helpful hint, then you should divide the smaller number by the larger number to find out what percentage of the larger number the smaller number makes up. Remember to move your decimal two places!

Example: What percent of 7.5 is .08?

.08 ÷ 7.5 = .1067 = 10.67%

Ecopolis © Prufrock Press Inc.

Permission is granted to photocopy or reproduce this page for single classroom use only.

63

ACTIVITY A

Answer the following questions, and show your work below. Round the result to the nearest tenth.

1. 125% of 850 is _____.
2. 84 is _____ percent of 220.
3. 70% of _____ is 300.
4. 56% of 78 is _____.
5. 310 is 70% of _____.
6. 25 is _____ percent of 80.
7. 62 is 94% of _____.
8. 27.5% of 150 is _____.
9. 74.6 is _____ percent of 160.
10. 452% of 86 is _____.

ACTIVITY B

Answer the following questions, and show your work below.

1. In 1991, about 60% of the 63,000,000 married couples in America had two incomes. About how many couples had two incomes?
2. Twenty years ago, 260,000 women made up 17.5% of all military personnel. How many military personnel were there 20 years ago?
3. Sales tax on a digital camera is $4.50 in a state where the sales tax rate is 9%. What is the cost of the digital camera?

ANSWER KEY

Activity A

1. 1062.5
2. 38.2%
3. 428.6
4. 43.7
5. 442.9
6. 31.3%
7. Approximately 66
8. 41.3
9. Approximately 46.6%
10. 388.72

Activity B

1. 37,800,000
2. Approximately 1,485,714
3. $50

HELPFUL HINTS

Head Honcho Campaign Speech
Helpful Hints: Resource Allocation

- *Resource allocation* is how you use Ecopolis's resources.
- *Resources* are the things that you have that can help you: five preferred seats; banks that each have beginning balances of $10,000; a government with a beginning balance of $10,000; and the power to *levy* (collect) taxes.
- *Allocations* are how you satisfy actual and potential needs, including meeting the salaries of elected officials, providing $500 stipends to poor Ecopolitans, possibly giving salaries to the assistants of politicians, and possibly paying interest on loans from the Ecomaster or private entrepreneurs (Jane Q. and John Q. Public).

Big Deal Campaign Speech
Helpful Hints: Wants vs. Needs

- Some basic human *needs* are food, water, and shelter.
- How will you satisfy Ecopolitans' needs by using your limited resources? (See a Head Honcho candidate to discuss what those resources are.)
- Remember that human *wants* are infinite—even once humans have everything they need, they will always want something else.
- Balance is the key. You must decide which human wants should be satisfied in order to result in the best possible situation for Ecopolitans.

Deep Pockets Campaign Speech
Helpful Hints: Taxation in a Market Economy

- Taxes are collected from *all* Ecopolitans.
- The amount Ecopolitans pay in taxes is based on their earnings and income, as well as whether they own preferred seating. Once elected, Ecopolis officials may decide to tax other things, too.
- Taxes are used to pay elected officials (and perhaps their assistants), to pay $500 stipends to poor Ecopolitans, to pay for police and fire protection, and to support schools.
- Who should decide how much Ecopolitans pay?
- Should the elected officials decide what is best for Ecopolitans?
- Would a *tax rebate* (getting money back after taxes) help some Ecopolitans purchase preferred seating?
- Would giving the Head Honcho an assistant (who would have to be paid) be a good thing or a bad thing for Ecopolis?

Lesson 4

Concepts

- Economic issues covered in Lesson 3
- Eye contact
- Projection
- Enunciation
- Tempo
- Organization

Materials

- Helpful Hints sheet from Lesson 3 (p. 67)
- Banker tutorial from Lesson 3 (pp. 47–62)
- Resource lesson from Lesson 3 (pp. 63–66)
- Elements of Public Speaking sheet (p. 71)
- Ballots (p. 72)

Student Objectives

Political office candidates, campaign managers, and bankers review the elements of effective public speaking: enunciation, projection, pace, and eye contact. Bankers teach their classmates the necessary information they have learned from the banker tutorial, and candidates teach their classmates what they have learned about economic issues via their campaign speeches.

Introduction

Review the elements of good public speaking by displaying and discussing the Elements of Public Speaking sheet.

Recognition

Students demonstrate an understanding of economic issues and public speaking elements by teaching their classmates what they learned in the banker tutorial and about the assigned campaign speech issues.

Application

Students implement what they have learned.

1. Bankers present their work, describing how and when to use each form.
2. Candidates deliver their speeches. Campaign managers can offer introductions and commentary, should you wish to allow them to demonstrate public speaking elements.

Problem Solving

Students demonstrate their knowledge and teach their fellow students.

1. Bankers review the forms and answer questions.
2. Candidates give their speeches.
3. Elections are held.

Grade-Level Expectations

The student:

- Recognizes the relationships between productivity and wages, and between wages and standards of living.
- Determines the opportunity cost of decisions.
- Identifies the factors of production.

Additional Notes

- Bankers have had 2 days to complete the banker tutorial, and the candidates have been researching and preparing their speeches. This is quite a load, and now is a good time to point out that you can allocate however much time is necessary for lessons. If you decide that your students need more time, you should extend this lesson. If, on the other hand, your students are ready more quickly, you might opt to complete this lesson in 1 day. Once the bankers have completed the banker tutorial, they should understand how students can acquire (if they can afford) preferred seating and use their savings accounts. Consider measuring understanding by asking the bankers to present to the class on the following topics:
  o How do Ecopolitans open savings accounts? How do these accounts work?
  o How do Ecopolitans calculate the daily interest they will receive by keeping their money in the bank overnight?

o   How should Ecopolitans calculate their daily preferred-seating expenses?

- You have several options for structuring this lesson. Generally, we recommend that you introduce each of the issues—resource allocation, wants vs. needs, and taxation in a market economy—to all of the students before the corresponding group of students makes their speeches. An alternative is to have campaign managers assist in the discussion of topics preceding candidates' speeches. Be aware, however, that this may not be advisable, as students are liable to campaign as they instruct. Because they have been focusing on the banker tutorial, bankers may have questions regarding the issues, so campaign managers could also assist with answering questions following the speeches.

- After all of the speeches have been delivered, distribute ballots and ask students to vote.

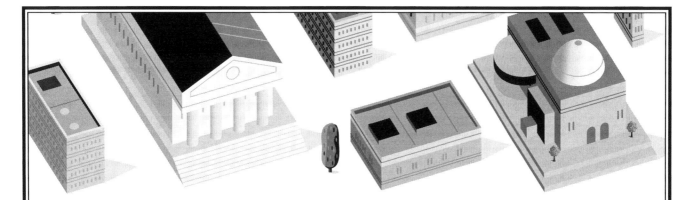

EYE CONTACT

Facing the audience and keeping your head up projects confidence; making eye contact with the audience keeps them interested.

PROJECTION

Speaking loudly, without yelling, gives the appearance of authority.

ENUNCIATION

Speaking clearly allows you to be understood and inspires confidence.

TEMPO

The pace of your speech should not be too fast, or people will be confused, and it should not be too slow, or people will be bored.

ORGANIZATION

Knowing your material, and in what order it will be presented, will allow you to deliver a speech that flows logically, and you will not get lost during your presentation.

BALLOTS

I want to vote for the following person to serve
as the **Head Honcho** (leader) of Ecopolis:

_____

_____

_____

☐

☐

☐

I want to vote for the following person to serve as
the **Big Deal** (assistant leader) of Ecopolis:

_____

_____

_____

☐

☐

☐

I want to vote for the following person to serve as
Deep Pockets (treasury chairperson) of Ecopolis:

_____

_____

_____

☐

☐

☐

Lesson 5A

Concepts

- Government taxation
- Earning interest
- Using a savings account

Materials

- Job descriptions (pp. 76–79)
- Earnings Statement sheet (p. 30)
- Tax Assessment sheet (individual; p. 80)
- Deep Pockets Tax Assessment sheet (group; p. 81)
- Bankers' forms (blank; pp. 82–84)
- Taxes, Taxes, Taxes sheet (p. 85)

Student Objective

Students develop the infrastructure of Ecopolis by assuming their roles and understanding them. They set up bank accounts and pay taxes, and preferred seating becomes available for sale.

Introduction

Announce the election results and distribute job descriptions. Review the processes needed for the simulation, making sure that students understand all they need to in order for Ecopolis to begin running.

Recognition

All students double check their Earnings Statement sheets with the Ecomaster. The elected officials introduce themselves to the Ecopolitans and explain their responsibilities.

Application

Students begin the simulation, demonstrating an understanding of their roles.

1. Ecopolitans proceed to the bank to set up savings accounts.
2. Ecopolitans compute their taxes and proceed to make payments to Deep Pockets.
3. Ecopolitans who have earned less than $1,000 proceed to the government to receive a $500 stipend.

Problem Solving

Students work to achieve the Ecopolitan dream.

1. Students develop strategies to help them map out paths to preferred seating ownership.
2. Students use their journal entries to organize their thoughts, planning, and resources.

Grade-Level Expectations

The student:

- Identifies the role of the individual in factors of production and markets.
- Explains how specialization and productivity are related.
- Recognizes the relationships between productivity and wages, and between wages and standards of living.
- Determines the opportunity cost of decisions.
- Identifies the factors of production.

Additional Notes

- In this lesson, students actually begin learning experientially. Don't be surprised if some students feel frustration. Bank lines will be long, and bankers may begin to realize that actually being a banker is much more challenging than merely learning about being a banker. We recommend that you assign all students to banks, so that each bank has an equal customer load. This can help avoid imbalances and hurt feelings. However, you can also use your discretion where this issue is concerned. We have had some students ask to switch banks because they considered one set of bankers more competent than the other.
- Students proceed to the banks to open savings accounts, and then to Deep Pockets to pay their income taxes. You may choose to allow them to pay their taxes prior to opening savings accounts. This is also acceptable; just ensure that students understand that they will have to pay taxes on any money they have earned thus far before purchasing preferred seating.
- Politicians may feel that they have down time, as there will likely be logjams at the banks. They do not yet have a complete view of their responsibili-

ties. The following lesson, Lesson 5B, will help occupy the politicians. You may choose to use this lesson once politicians have opened savings accounts and paid their taxes, should they seem unoccupied. They will need to make speeches in Lesson 7, so if they begin learning now about the topics that they will need to speak about later on, then they will be much better prepared. Thus, they can begin researching topics they will have to know about while the Ecopolitans and bankers are occupied. We suggest making the speech an out-of-class assignment that the political figures can begin in class.

- The provided tax assessment forms are used by students to calculate what they owe the government in taxes. Throughout the unit, they should pay taxes each time they make money to avoid losing track of things. In addition to the individual form, there is a group form that Deep Pockets uses to record tax payments. One of Deep Pockets's responsibilities is to verify that each taxpaying Ecopolitan has completed the necessary paperwork correctly (the dreaded audit). Each student calculates and pays his or her taxes to Deep Pockets. Deep Pockets signs each customer's individual tax form to indicate that taxes have been paid. Students then proceed to the bank to open a savings account. If a student has not earned at least $1,000, then he or she is paid a $500 stipend by the government. This happens twice, once in Lesson 5 and again in Lesson 7. Thus, Deep Pockets has a lot of responsibility. Once this becomes clear, the elected officials can decide whether and how they want to address this. We have had many classes appoint an assistant to Deep Pockets, to be paid out of government funds.

- When banks make loans, promissory notes are used to help customers keep track of interest payments. Daily interest payments (on the outstanding amount owed on the bank loan) must be made to retain possession of preferred seating. Otherwise, a foreclosure happens, the Big Deal is alerted, and there is an auction to sell the preferred seat to the highest bidder.

- Emphasize to students that although they are only obligated to pay interest payments, they should also pay back the principal as quickly as possible. This will make their interest payments lower.

- Elected officials are told that they have the power to raise taxes. The provided materials use set guidelines regarding income taxes, but as the unit progresses, elected officials may cut taxes, create new ones, or raise taxes. (In our experience, elected officials are hesitant to alter the given income tax rates.)

- Some students may be ready to begin creating jobs and goods and services to sell. Forms to help them accomplish this are included in Lesson 6, where this aspect of the simulation is explained further. (Every time students make money, they must pay taxes on their earnings.) Materials needed to run the simulation are found in both Lesson 5A and Lesson 6, and we have divided them into materials that students will need right away (in Lesson 5A) and those that students will likely not need for a little while (Lesson 6).

HEAD HONCHO (LEADER) JOB DESCRIPTION

Congratulations! You have been elected by a group of your peers to serve as the Head Honcho of Ecopolis for this unit. You have campaigned skillfully, will earn a $5,000 salary, and are faced with a daunting task.

You must balance the needs and wants of the consumers as they work toward ownership of preferred seating, and you must also maintain the health of the economy for all Ecopolitans.

Here are some of the questions you must ask yourself:

1. Will consumers' acquisition of preferred seating lead to shortages (not enough preferred seats) in Ecopolis?
2. Will consumers be able to afford property taxes on their preferred seats?
3. How will consumers who have been unable to acquire enough resources to buy a seat be encouraged to continue striving to achieve the great Ecopolitan dream of preferred seating ownership?
4. Will you buy yourself a preferred seat?
5. Will you have enough tax revenue to pay the political employees? These include Deep Pockets (the treasury chairperson and tax collector, who gets a $2,000 salary); the Big Deal (the assistant leader, who gets a $3,000 salary); and yourself—who gets a $5,000 salary.
6. How will you work with banks to enable more consumers to acquire preferred seating?
7. How will you balance the demand for preferred seating with the available supply of preferred seating?

These are only a few of the issues you will face! Don't forget that you have the Big Deal and Deep Pockets to advise and assist you in managing Ecopolis.

Good luck! You will be earning every penny of your salary.

BIG DEAL (ASSISTANT LEADER)
JOB DESCRIPTION

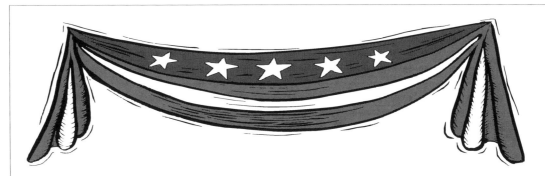

Congratulations! You have been elected by a group of your peers to serve as the Big Deal of Ecopolis for this unit. You have campaigned skillfully, will earn a $3,000 salary, and are faced with a daunting task.

As the Big Deal, you bear the responsibility of assisting Head Honcho whenever help and advice are needed to guide the economy.

In addition, you have some specific responsibilities, including the following:

1. You must help the bank assist the Ecopolitans. Are banks providing John Q. and Jane Q. Public with adequate account services? Are bank loan policies providing all residents of Ecopolis the opportunity to buy preferred seating? Make recommendations to the Head Honcho that would improve bank services.

2. You must act as an advocate for John Q. and Jane Q. Public. Is there an adequate supply of preferred seating in Ecopolis to meet the public's demand? How can you help consumers attain their goal of preferred seating? Keep track of what you can do to satisfy the needs of the public. It is your responsibility to provide a stipend of $500 to any person who has been unfortunate and not earned at least $1,000 on his or her earning statement.

3. Banks are paid a return of 4% on deposits held overnight. You must see to it that the Fed (the Ecomaster) makes that payment at the beginning of each class.

4. Jane Q. and John Q. Public may come to you for help and advice. You are their chief advocate. You will also approve job proposals for them.

5. In addition to completing your official duties, you will have to decide whether you will purchase a preferred seat for yourself.

Don't forget that you have the Head Honcho to rely on for guidance. You can also depend on Deep Pockets to make money available to you so that you can pay for the obligations of Ecopolis.

Good luck! You'll be earning every penny of your salary.

DEEP POCKETS (TREASURY CHAIRPERSON) JOB DESCRIPTION

Congratulations! You have been elected by a group of your peers to serve as Deep Pockets (the treasury chairperson and tax collector) of Ecopolis for this unit. You have campaigned skillfully, have earned a $2,000 salary, and are faced with a daunting task.

As Deep Pockets, you bear the responsibility of assisting the Head Honcho (leader) whenever help and advice are needed to guide the economy. Additionally, you are to support and execute the requests of the Big Deal (assistant leader).

In addition, you have some specific responsibilities:

1. Act as the *fiscal* (dealing with money) agent for Ecopolis. You must collect enough money to keep Ecopolis operating.

> **Earnings Tax:** A tax to be paid by every Ecopolitan and recorded on the Tax Assessment sheet. Those who earn more than $5,000 have a 30% tax rate. Those who earn between $2,000 and $5,000 have a 20% tax rate. Those who earn between $1,000 and $2,000 have a 10% tax rate. Those who earn less than $1,000 have a 0% tax rate and receive a $500 stipend from Ecopolis.
>
> **Property Tax:** Ecopolitans who purchase preferred seating will pay a property tax of 10% of the purchase price of the seat, which is due at the time of purchase.
>
> **Bank Tax:** Every time a bank makes a loan to an Ecopolitan that results in the purchase of preferred seating, the bank pays a fee of $100 to Ecopolis.

2. Oversee the banks.

Don't forget that you have the Head Honcho to depend on for guidance and that the Big Deal will be needing money from you to meet the obligations of Ecopolitans.

In addition to performing your official duties, you will have to decide whether you will purchase a preferred seat for yourself.

Good luck! You'll be earning every penny of your salary.

JOHN Q. PUBLIC AND JANE Q. PUBLIC
(CITIZENS OF ECOPOLIS)
JOB DESCRIPTION

Welcome to Ecopolis. As members of the public, you are the engine that powers everything that will happen in Ecopolis.

In the past several days, you have elected officials whose task it is to satisfy your needs and wants by guiding the economy through challenges that everyone will face.

The Head Honcho, the leader, has the responsibility of guiding the economy. The Big Deal, the assistant leader, will serve as your advocate and contact person to the government. Deep Pockets, the treasury chairperson and tax collector, will collect income and property taxes so that the government can provide you with services. Money Bags, the bankers, will provide you with the opportunity to borrow money so that you can buy preferred seating, if you wish, and to open savings accounts. The success of each and every one of these officials depends in part upon *your* success.

Your goal is to become as wealthy as possible so that you can improve the standard of living for you and your family.

To do this, you should try to purchase preferred seating. You should also increase your earnings by developing a job for yourself that will in some way help the people of Ecopolis—that will satisfy their needs or wants. To create a job for yourself, you will be able to submit a proposal to the Big Deal.

You can also try to increase your earnings by performing research for your teacher and educating your fellow Ecopolitans about the way the economy works. For this, you will be able to submit a proposal form for your teacher.

Good luck! Go forth, spend money, and be prosperous!

Ecopolis © Prufrock Press Inc.

Permission is granted to photocopy or reproduce this page for single classroom use only.

79

TAX ASSESSMENT

DATE	TOTAL EARNINGS (from Earnings Statement) A	TAX % x A = B B	BALANCE (to deposit into savings) A – B = C C

ECOPOLIS TAX RATES
Earnings > $5,000 = 30% Tax Rate
$3,000 < Earnings < $5,000 = 20% Tax Rate
$1,000 < Earnings < $3,000 = 10% Tax Rate
Earnings < $1000 = 0% Tax Rate; $500 Stipend

DEEP POCKETS TAX ASSESSMENT

NAME	DATE	TOTAL EARNINGS (from Earnings Statement) A	TAX % % x A = B B	BALANCE (total government funds) C + or − B C
X	X	X	X	$10,000
			TOTAL TAX (add values in Column B)	

Banker: _____

Customer: _____ Date: _____

ECOPOLIS SAVINGS ACCOUNT FORM
(Banker Copy)

Day	A Balance	B Deposits	C Withdrawals	D Interest (2%) $.02 \times (A + (B - C)) =$	E Final balance $A + B + D - C$
1					
2					
3					
4					
Totals					

Ecopolis © Prufrock Press Inc.

Customer: _____

Banker: _____ Date: _____

ECOPOLIS SAVINGS ACCOUNT FORM
(Customer Copy)

Day	A Balance	B Deposits	C Withdrawals	D Interest (2%) .02 x (A + (B – C))=	E Final balance A + B + D – C
1					
2					
3					
4					
Totals					

Banker:_____

Customer: _____ Date: _____

BANK DAILY SUMMARY

Transaction	A Balance	B Total deposits (from Ecopolis Savings Accounts)	C Total withdrawals (from Ecopolis Savings Accounts)	D Bank earnings (4%) $(A + (B - C)) \times .04 =$	E Total interest expenses (from Ecopolis Savings Accounts Column D)	F Final balance $A + B + D - C - E =$
1						
2						
3						
4						
Totals						

TAXES, TAXES, TAXES

Step 1: How am I doing?

Total savings _____

+ Preferred seating down payment _____

+ Value of any other assets _____

= Total assets _____

Step 2: What is my tax rate?

Total Assets (TA)

[   ]

ECOPOLIS TAX RATES

TA > $5,000 = 30% Tax Rate

$3,000 < **TA** < $5,000 = 20% Tax Rate

$1,000 < **TA** < $3,000.00 = 10% Tax Rate

TA < $1,000 = 0% Tax Rate; $500 Stipend

Tax Rate

[   ]

Step 3: How much money have I made since the last time I paid taxes?

Savings account interest _____

+ Earnings from homework, classwork, good deeds, and so on _____

+ Earnings from jobs _____

+ Earnings from teaching _____

+ Earnings from miscellaneous (specify) _____

_____

= Total earnings _____

Step 4: How much do I owe the government?

Tax rate x Total earnings = Money owed

_____ x _____ = _____

Lesson 5B

Concepts

- Supply and demand
- Scarcity and wants vs. needs
- Government taxation in a market economy

Materials

- Head Honcho speech assignment (p. 88)
- Head Honcho guiding questions (pp. 89–90; answer key on pp. 91–92)
- Big Deal speech assignment (p. 93)
- Big Deal guiding questions (p. 94)
- Deep Pockets speech assignment (p. 95)
- Deep Pockets guiding questions (p. 96)

Student Objective

Students playing politicians learn about the relationships between supply and demand, wants vs. needs, and the role of the government in a market economy by researching assigned speech topics.

Introduction

Distribute speech assignments to all of the politicians and explain that they will be making speeches on these topics to Ecopolitans in a few days. Tell the politicians that if they want to, they may hire ghostwriters to help them with their research. Make it clear that they must use their own salaries, rather than government funds, to pay their helpers!

Recognition

The politicians demonstrate an understanding of the speech assignment by repeating the lesson objective to the teacher and by asking relevant questions.

Application

Politicians (and their ghostwriters, if the politicians choose to hire them) brainstorm for their speeches and gather data.

Problem Solving

Politicians will deliver their speeches at the beginning of Lesson 7.

Grade-Level Expectations

The student:
- Explains how specialization and productivity are related.
- Determines the opportunity cost of decisions.
- Recognizes that shortage and surplus affect the price and availability of goods and services.

Additional Notes

- Students are to use the provided guiding questions to help decide in what directions to take their research. They may point out that they have just made speeches on similar issues, but they will discover as the unit progresses that they have additional material to speak about, and that they must investigate related concepts they had not considered. That research can take the form of running Internet keyword searches; using human resources (e.g., parents, other relatives, administrators, other teachers in your school); borrowing periodicals from the library; visiting the media center; and so on.
- It can be tempting to jump in and teach when students are researching issues, particularly those with which they are unfamiliar. Use your judgment in terms of whether you assist the students or provide additional guidelines. It is often interesting to see how students' notions of these issues evolve as they participate in the unit. Because the Head Honcho's guiding questions may require a bit of teacher guidance, we have included an answer key for those questions.

MEMO _____

To: The Head Honcho
From: The Ecomaster

Dear H. H.,

It has come to my attention that the citizens of Ecopolis are upset about the rising price of preferred seats. You must make a speech very soon to explain the reasons that these prices are going up.

You may want to hire writers to help you research the economic issues of supply and demand to figure out the answers to the preferred seating question, being that you do not have much time to prepare. Your writers will expect to be paid for their services, but you cannot use government funds to pay them—you must use your own money. I am sure this will not be a problem, as you are scheduled to receive your second salary payment of $5,000 right after the speech.

Because this salary is paid using tax revenue collected by Deep Pockets, the Ecopolitans are paying your salary. You must explain this economic issue very clearly for them—especially if you want to be reelected. After all, that's why you get paid the big bucks!

Signed,

PREPARING FOR YOUR SPEECH (HEAD HONCHO)

As the Head Honcho, you must explain to Ecopolitans how the forces of supply and demand work together to arrive at an *equilibrium price*, the price at which all preferred seats are sold and everybody is happy.

Use the following questions to prepare a speech, to be delivered in a few days, explaining to Ecopolitans how the forces of supply and demand dictate the number of preferred seats that exist in Ecopolis.

1. Explain what a demand curve is. Why it is sloping downward, from left to right, in the following diagram?

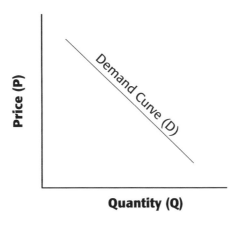

2. Explain what a supply curve is. Why is it sloping upward, from left to right, in the following diagram?

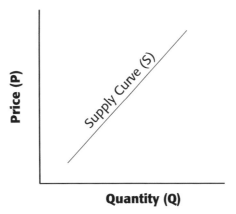

3. Explain how forces of supply and demand work together to arrive at the equilibrium price (PЄ; the price at which preferred seats are sold) where everyone is happy.

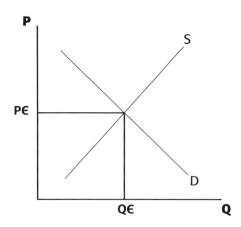

Ecopolis © Prufrock Press Inc.

PREPARING FOR YOUR SPEECH
(HEAD HONCHO)
ANSWER KEY

1. As price decreases, quantity demanded increases. In the figure below, at price P_1 quantity Q_1 is demanded. As price falls to P_2, quantity Q_2 is demanded. Therefore, as price decreases, the quantity demanded increases.

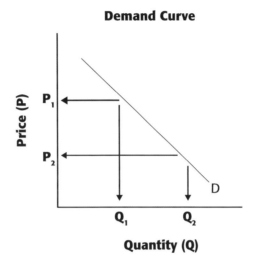

Demand Curve

2. In this example, at price P_1 quantity Q_1 is being supplied. As the price increases to P_2, quantity Q_2 is being supplied. Therefore, as price increases, the quantity supplied increases.

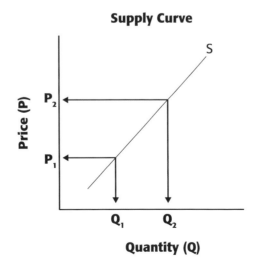

Supply Curve

Ecopolis © Prufrock Press Inc.

91

Permission is granted to photocopy or reproduce this page for single classroom use only.

3. We begin at P_e, Q_e, where the exact number of seats being supplied is also being demanded. More Ecopolitans demand preferred seating, however, causing a shift in demand from D_1 to D_2. The citizens wanted more, and they got more, but they had to pay more to get what they wanted.

Equilibrium Price Curve

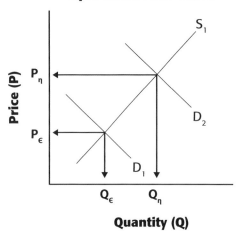

MEMO

To: The Big Deal
From: The Ecomaster

Dear B. D.,

It would seem that many of our citizens are unhappy with the economic structure of our community. Many Ecopolitans have complained that they are unable to buy a preferred seat. It seems that they feel entitled to this privilege. It is your job to explain to them that there is a difference between wants and needs. It is impossible for anyone to have all of their wants met, because wants are infinite. Our economy, however, is not infinite!

It is up to you to reassure our citizens that the government cares for them, but cannot be held responsible to satisfy their wants—rather, the government should help Ecopolitans make sure that their needs are met. The government has to make hard choices about which of our citizens' needs are most important. Therefore, citizens must be part of the solution.

This is a very important speech—your future political career hangs in the balance! You may want to hire ghostwriters to help you research the economic issue of wants vs. needs. You will, of course, have to pay them with your own money, not government money. However, I assume this will not be problematic, as you are scheduled to receive your $3,000 salary again soon. Tax money—and therefore, Ecopolitans—pay this salary, so you have to explain yourself well!

Signed,

Ecomaster

PREPARING FOR YOUR SPEECH (BIG DEAL)

As the Big Deal, you will need to prepare a speech, to be delivered in several days, explaining to Ecopolitans why the satisfaction of all human wants is not possible in a finite economy. You may use a ghostwriter to assist, provided you pay out of your own pocket. Use the following questions to prepare a speech, to be delivered in several days, explaining to Ecopolitans why the satisfaction of all humans wants is not possible in a finite economy.

1. What is the nature of human need? What do human beings need in order to survive?

2. What is the nature of human wants? Do human beings ever stop wanting things? What sorts of things do human beings want?

3. What is scarcity? Is scarcity the result of an economy not being able to provide enough goods and services to satisfy all people's needs? What about all of their wants?

4. How can scarcity be eliminated? Can supply ever be increased enough to eliminate scarcity?

MEMO _____

To: Deep Pockets
From: The Ecomaster

Dear D. P.,

There has been much grumbling from the citizens of Ecopolis. They are upset about the amount of money they must pay in taxes. Questions are being raised about why they must pay the salaries of elected officials. You must put an end to this discontent before it gets out of hand!

You may hire ghostwriters to assist you if you wish, but you will have to pay them out of your own pocket, rather than using government money. This should not be a problem, because you will soon be receiving another salary payment of $2,000. It is essential that you explain to the citizens what government services are doing for them, as well as why everyone must contribute to these services. Without their tax revenue, the entire economy would collapse—and what is more, your salary could not be paid! You must explain why taxes cost the amounts they do, and justify the existence of taxes for the citizens of Ecopolis. Good luck!

Signed,

Name:_____ Date: _____

PREPARING FOR YOUR
SPEECH (DEEP POCKETS)

As Deep Pockets, you will need to prepare a speech, to be delivered in several days, to explain to Ecopolitans why the government services that you provide are necessary for the successful operation of Ecopolis. You may hire ghostwriters to assist you, but remember that you must pay them out of pocket, rather than using government funds. Use the following questions to prepare a speech:

1. Why is the $500 stipend (paid to less fortunate Ecopolitans) necessary for these citizens to succeed?

2. How is your speech (along with the speech made by the Head Honcho and the Big Deal) helpful to Ecopolitans? What responsibilities do the Ecopolitans have?

3. How have the government's establishment and funding of banks been helpful to Ecopolitans?

4. How has providing Ecopolitans with equal opportunities been helpful?

Lesson 6

Concepts

- Individual responsibility and resources
- Supply and demand
- Wants vs. needs

Materials

- Employment Proposal sheet (p. 100)
- Education Proposal sheet (p. 101)
- Promissory Note sheet (p. 102)
- Notice of Foreclosure sheet (p. 103)
- *The Rug Tug Times*, Issue 1 (p. 104)

Student Objective

Students continue to participate in Ecopolis, generating income and addressing challenges.

Introduction

Review how to be a successful citizen of Ecopolis, and discuss any issues that have arisen thus far in the simulation.

Recognition

Students write in their journals, explaining how they plan to achieve success in Ecopolis.

Application

Students continue to strive for the Ecopolitan dream.

1. At this point, Ecopolis is fully functional.
2. Taxes are being assessed and paid.
3. Savings accounts are open and earning interest for customers and banks.
4. Preferred seating continues to be bought and sold.
5. Citizens continue to earn capital.
6. Banks and government continue executing their responsibilities.

Problem Solving

The teacher and students debrief about the experience to help clarify the day's events.

1. At the end of class, the teacher leads a discussion. What happened? What were students' reactions to various events? What will students do differently tomorrow?
2. Students return to their journals and reflect on how the day went for them, focusing on why certain things happened and how they can alter their courses the next day.

Grade-Level Expectations

The student:

- Identifies the role of the individual in factor and product markets.
- Explains how specialization and productivity are related.
- Determines the opportunity cost of decisions.
- Recognizes that shortage and surplus affect the price and availability of goods and services.

Additional Notes

- Students who are not politicians or bankers continue to earn money in various ways. You can still distribute monetary rewards for good behavior and other behaviors, as in Lesson 1 and the beginning of the simulation. (You do not have to continue doing this, however.) Students can also submit proposals for employment, which are subject to your approval. We have had students produce a newspaper to rival *The Rug Tug Times*; act as substitute bankers should bankers be absent (yes, some students are able to pick up on the skills necessary to serve as bankers despite not having completed the banker tutorial); act as judges to resolve disputes as they arise; and act as assistants to Deep Pockets during the tax collection process. The possibilities are limitless, and students often surprise us with their creativity. Students can also complete teaching proposals (also subject to your approval) asking for payment in return for educating one or many classmates. A student could serve as a tutor, for example, or students could teach their classmates about passions or hobbies by way of a mini-lecture or presentation. Who pays the student depends on the goods or services rendered. Students can buy from or hire one another as individuals, the elected officials can hire students, or the Ecomaster can pay a student if he or she has something to offer the entire class. There is much flexibility where hiring and payment are concerned.

- Do not be surprised if you hear some grumbling about high taxes and about stipends being paid to Ecopolitans who are underperforming. This is expected and will be addressed by the politicians' speeches in Lesson 7. You may distribute the first issue of *The Rug Tug Times* at any point in order to set the stage for politicians' speeches in Lesson 7. This issue reminds students of elected officials' salaries—at this point, students will know enough to be very offended by the disparity in earnings between themselves and elected officials.

- Foreclosures may be appearing, affecting Ecopolitans who have acquired preferred seating and can no longer afford this luxury. To conduct a bank auction, the Head Honcho delivers the Notice of Foreclosure sheet to the Ecomaster, who announces the time and place of the foreclosure auction (e.g., "The auction of the Cushioned Rolling Chair will occur at 10:45 at Megabucks Bank"). At the specified time and place, the bank will accept bids on the seat. Depending on the class dynamic, you may choose to run the auction as a silent one, using sealed bids, or you may use a more public bidding process, complete with an auctioneer and bidding cards. See the banker tutorial for a numerical example of a foreclosure process.

- It is up to you how many days to keep students in this phase of the simulation. We recommend that you remain on Lesson 6, allowing students to experiment with their roles and actions in Ecopolis, for at least 2 days. If the students are actively engaged in developing their economy and pursuing preferred seating, you may wish to let them continue this lesson for a few additional days. *The Rug Tug Times* was so named because the issue it raises "pulls the rug out" from under the fledgling economy. When the economy is challenged, the students are given the opportunity to problem solve and to think creatively. Thus, you should wait until students have a fairly good grasp on the workings of Ecopolis before introducing this challenge with the second issue of the newspaper.

- Try as you might, some students may be difficult to engage. You might consider putting together an economic stimulus package, which could include grade incentives or job assignments, in addition to any other ideas you can think of that would be useful in your class.

Name:_____ Date: _____

EMPLOYMENT PROPOSAL

Please write a complete description of your proposed service or product:

_____

_____

_____

_____

_____

_____

_____

_____

Below, please describe the factors of production that will be required to generate your proposed service or product. List any costs, materials, or other considerations that would be needed for production.

Labor: _____

Materials: _____

Delivery: _____

Total cost: _____

Proposed consumer price: _____

This idea was approved on _____ (date) by the following:

_____

Head Honcho

_____

Big Deal

_____

Ecomaster

EDUCATION PROPOSAL

Please write a complete description of your proposed topic:

_____

_____

_____

_____

_____

_____

_____

_____

Below, please describe the factors of production that will be required to teach your proposed topic. List any costs, materials, or other considerations that would be needed for you to teach.

Labor: _____

Materials: _____

Method of delivering information
(e.g., poster, overhead projector): _____

Proposed date of delivery: _____

Total cost of service: _____

This idea was approved on _____ (date) by the following:

_____
Ecomaster

Promissory Note

I, _____ , borrowed $ _____

from the _____ bank on _____ .

Date

I promise to repay the bank in full at a rate of _____ % interest by the end of

Ecopolis.

_____   _____
Bank President   Borrower

Promissory Note

I, _____ , borrowed $ _____

from the _____ bank on _____ .

Date

I promise to repay the bank in full at a rate of _____ % interest by the end of

Ecopolis.

_____   _____
Bank President   Borrower

Promissory Note

I, _____ , borrowed $ _____

from the _____ bank on _____ .

Date

I promise to repay the bank in full at a rate of _____ % interest by the end of

Ecopolis.

_____   _____
Bank President   Borrower

NOTICE OF FORECLOSURE

It is heretofore declared that _____,
current owner of preferred seating location _____,
is unable to make interest payments on his or her property loan. Therefore,
ownership will revert to the bank with the signature of this Notice. This
document will serve to notify the authorities that the abovementioned
property has been foreclosed upon. The property will be auctioned off to
the highest bidder at an auction conducted by the bank. The proceeds
from this auction will be used to repay the bank's loan, and any profit
realized above the value of the debt will revert to the abovementioned
owner.

The current value of the property is $ _____ .
The current value of the debt is $ _____ .

_____   _____
Bank President   Date

_____   _____
Property Owner   Date

Political Bigwigs Must Explain Themselves!

Ecopolitans will soon have the opportunity to hear their representatives speak on relevant economic issues that have been creating discontent in Ecopolis. Many citizens have been heard complaining about a variety of issues, including the fact that preferred seating costs continue to rise, making it ever more difficult for regular folks to achieve the Ecopolitan dream.

More and more people have been discontented with how much they have been able to earn, achieve, and buy. Furthermore, an increasing number of people are stating that the politicians must offer some kind of justification for all of the programs the government offers—programs that are paid with citizens' tax dollars. Some say that if they did not need to pay taxes, they could buy preferred seating without a problem.

To address this growing discontent, the politicians of Ecopolis plan to make speeches tackling the issues. The Head Honcho will reportedly discuss the issue of preferred seating costs, hopefully explaining why prices continue to skyrocket. The Big Deal will follow up with a speech addressing citizens' concern that no matter how hard they try, they cannot get everything that they want. Deep Pockets will close the presentation by outlining and justifying the services that the government supplies, including the stimulus aid given to Ecopolitans who earn below the poverty line. There will be a question and answer session following the speeches.

Many citizens are very curious to hear what the politicians have to say. One representative from the government office, who requested to remain anonymous, said that protests against the government, rising seating costs, and high taxes are growing. "People want to know where all of the money is going—especially because the Head Honcho isn't exactly strapped for cash."

In terms of salary payments, top-tier government officials earn much more than the average Ecopolitan; and these officials are slated to be paid again directly following their speeches. *The Rug Tug Times* has confirmed that Deep Pockets pulls in a cool $2,000, whereas Big Deal earns a reported $3,000. Head Honcho, on the other hand, makes a whopping $5,000.

Weather update:

Sunny skies and strong wind are in the forecast for our area, along with record high temperatures. The afternoon brings a 30% chance of showers.

Lesson 7

Concepts

- Global interdependence
- Elements of public speaking

Materials

- Crisis edition of *The Rug Tug Times* (p. 108)

Student Objective

Students extend their understanding of the interconnectedness of economic events by experiencing a crisis situation.

Introduction

Begin this lesson by having the Head Honcho, the Big Deal, and Deep Pockets deliver their speeches. After their speeches, they will receive their second salary payments. Then, call the students together to inform them that a disaster has struck Ecopolis. Circulate the second issue of *The Rug Tug Times*.

Recognition

A group forum is led by the Head Honcho to consult with citizens and gain information. Students should demonstrate that they recognize the pertinent economic concepts in this forum.

Application

The Head Honcho, the Big Deal, and Deep Pockets take charge of the situation.
1. Working with the citizens, they propose a solution to the problem.
2. They figure out what they must do to execute their solution.
3. They delegate tasks as necessary.

4. The Big Deal keeps in contact with Ecopolitans and informs the Head Honcho of their concerns, complaints, and suggestions.

Problem Solving

Each student should engage on an individual level with the crisis.

1. After the crisis has been addressed, each student should complete a journal entry reflecting on the situation.
2. Students should describe what steps were taken, as well as assessing how effective those steps were.
3. Students should reflect on what they would have done differently to address the crisis.

Grade-Level Expectations

The student:

- Identifies the role of the individual in factor and product markets.
- Explains how specialization and productivity are related.
- Recognizes the relationships between productivity and wages, and between wages and standards of living.
- Determines the opportunity cost of decisions.
- Recognizes that shortage and surplus affect the price and availability of goods and services.

Additional Notes:

- Only the most astute students will have realized that every time a preferred seat is purchased, money leaves Ecopolis and is funneled to the Ecomaster, who represents foreign nations. This, of course, underscores to students the concept of global interdependence. Ecopolis will be imbalanced if money flows out without coming in.
- You may have to help students better understand the nature of the crisis. Once they do, it can be tempting for you to intervene and help them solve the problem, but this would be robbing them of the valuable opportunity to investigate possible solutions for themselves. They might try raising taxes, which would likely fail due to insufficient money remaining in the system. They may ask for a loan from the Ecomaster, which could have dire long-term consequences. Others may come up with the possibility of issuing government bonds, effectively borrowing money from themselves. The problems students will face imitate the problems we face today in our global economy. One of the most interesting features of this unit is that it could end in many different ways, not all of them providing an entirely satisfactory solution to the crisis. In this way, students are exposed to the pitfalls and challenges of our modern global economy.

- It is effective to impose some sort of time limit in which students must solve the problem, which is up to your judgment; this not only imitates real-life crises, but also makes students more compelled to act quickly.
- An economic failure in Ecopolis should not be equated with a failure to learn. The goal is to teach economic concepts, not to create and sustain a viable economy.

THE RUG TUG TIMES

Local and World News Brought to YOU!　　　　　　　　Volume 1, Issue 2

Where's the Money?

The Rug Tug Times has uncovered some serious problems with the way the government has been handling resources. According to several reliable sources, in order to make preferred seating available, the government has been exporting factors of production, meaning that for every seat that is bought, money leaves Ecopolis. Ecopolitans pay huge quantities of money for these seats—and in addition, for every seat purchased, property taxes are paid.

Citizens have the right to know where their money is going. Where is the money? Every time a preferred seat is sold, a greater amount of money leaves Ecopolis. Upon hearing this news, many Ecopolitans are quite concerned, wondering if Ecopolis is getting poorer—and if so, how it will continue to sustain itself. Moreover, many citizens want to know whether the public officials had any knowledge of these events, calling for answers from the Head Honcho, the Big Deal, and Deep Pockets. If the politicians *did* know about the situation, then they have a lot of explaining to do. Even if they were unaware of the situation, solutions must be found in order to avert disaster in Ecopolis.

Weather update:

Thunderstorms and record low temperatures are headed our way. Expect showers in the morning, followed by strong winds and a cold front.

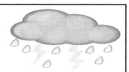

Lesson 8

Concepts

- Self-reflection
- Self-assessment
- Evidence-based assessment
- Creating strong visual aids

Materials

- Final journal entry (pp. 112–113)
- Final rubric (p. 114)
- Final Interview Preparation Tips sheet (p. 115)
- Economics Postassessment sheet (pp. 116–117; answer key on pp. 24–25)
- Complete the Statements sheet (pp. 118–119)
- Poster board and poster-making materials

Student Objective

In an interview with the teacher, the student demonstrates what he or she has learned in the simulation.

Introduction

Discuss the importance of reflection in self-assessment, including how it complements learning and how important it is to offer evidence of progress.

Recognition

In their interviews, students make specific statements reflecting on their experiences in Ecopolis, and they use economics vocabulary and appropriate language to describe their experiences.

Application

Prepare students to assess their progress in the unit.

1. Review the final rubric with students.
2. Have students complete the final journal entry in order to provide evidence of progress.
3. Have students work through the Complete the Statements sheet. (The items on this sheet are stated in the same language used in the unit's grade-level expectations.)

Problem Solving

Students communicate what they have learned in Ecopolis.

1. Each student creates a visual aid that represents his or her work and progress in Ecopolis.
2. Students interview with the teacher to offer evidence of their progress. If you wish to extend the simulation, you can also have students argue for whether they should remain in their current roles or whether they should be allowed to serve in a different capacity. (See Additional Notes.)
3. Students complete the Economics Postassessment sheet (the same as the Economics Preassessment sheet in Lesson 1) while they are waiting for their interviews.

Grade-Level Expectations

The student:

- Identifies the role of the individual in factor and product markets.
- Explains how specialization and productivity are related.
- Recognizes the relationships between productivity and wages, and between wages and standards of living.
- Determines the opportunity cost of decisions.
- Recognizes that shortage and surplus affect the price and availability of goods and services.

Additional Notes

- This lesson allows students to debrief about their experiences during Ecopolis, which will facilitate their learning in addition to providing you with information with which to assess them.
- On the first day, have students prepare for an exit interview by listing their successes and challenges. If you elect to end the unit here, you can ask them to reflect on whether they were satisfied in their roles, or whether they wish they could have played different roles. If you are extending the unit, you can ask them whether they might like to play new roles.

- Depending on how you conduct the interviews (see following note), you should instruct the students to prepare visual aids to highlight their experiences. We also recommend that you distribute the provided rubric to students so that they know what criteria will be used to judge them.
- On the second day, the interviews could take several forms. You can hold actual interviews—either by yourself, or with an administrator, a teaching assistant, a gifted resource specialist, and so on—or you could set up a fair so that Ecopolitans have stations where they can set up visual aids and discuss their progress with circulating judges.
- The Complete the Statements sheet can be used along with the other materials provided as a measure of student progress. In addition to using the Economics Postassessment sheet, you can use the Banker Selection Qualifier and the Student Context Rubric included in the Appendix. Thus, you have many ways with which to measure student progress.

We hope that you have enjoyed Ecopolis! By now, students have learned a great deal about our economic system through discovery and hands-on experiences. We hope that they were active and engaged learners—and that you went home smiling.

Name:_____ Date: _____

FINAL JOURNAL ENTRY

My role in Ecopolis was
_____

My ending balance, including property values, was
_____

Accomplishments:

_____

_____

_____

_____

_____

_____

I feel that I was very successful in . . .

_____

_____

_____

_____

_____

_____

_____

Name:_____ Date: _____

I wish that I had worked harder . . .

_____

_____

_____

_____

_____

_____

_____

Name:_____ Date: _____

FINAL RUBRIC

	C.E.O. (3 points)	V.I.P (2 points)	TRAINEE (1 point)	SCORE
ACCOUNTING	Accurately maintains all bank accounts, checks for agreement with all bank records, and records all expenditures.	Generally maintains accounts, but has several mathematical errors in accounting that disagree with the bank's records.	Does not track expenditures or earnings, and depends on the bank to maintain records.	
INCREASED EARNINGS	Successfully develops ways to generate income through research, employment, or services offered.	Generates some income through savings account interest. Attempts to offer services, but they are not utilized by other Ecopolitans.	Neglects to open a savings account. Is eligible for a $500 stipend. Is unable to generate earnings through offering a service or product in Ecopolis.	
USE OF RESOURCES	Balances wants and needs and makes constructive choices. This Ecopolitan is able to purchase desired resources, including preferred seating.	Obtains a preferred seat or other desired resources, but may be forced to sell them or foreclose due to flawed resource allocation.	Is unable to qualify for a loan or acquire resources.	
LEADERSHIP	Makes and shares decisions in such a way that others are drawn to make the same decision. Is able to sell a service to seem like a need, rather than a want.	Makes decisions that benefit self, but is unable to sway others to same point of view.	Is unable to make sound economic decisions. Makes no contribution to the economic well-being of Ecopolis.	

FINAL INTERVIEW PREPARATION TIPS

Bankers

- Dress the part of a banker.
- Complete all worksheets, and rewrite them if necessary so that they are legible.
- Create an attractive poster displaying the following:
    o Your bank's name and logo.
    o A one- or two-paragraph summary explaining the strategies you used to serve your customers.
    o A one- or two-paragraph summary detailing how you used your position as a banker to benefit the economy.

Politicians

- Dress the part of a politician.
- Complete all worksheets, and rewrite them if necessary so that they are legible.
- Create an attractive poster displaying the following:
    o Your name and title.
    o A one- or two-paragraph summary explaining the strategies you used to keep the economy moving forward.
    o A one- or two-paragraph summary detailing the greatest challenges you faced in your Ecopolitical life.

Ecopolitans

- Complete all worksheets, and rewrite them if necessary so that they are legible.
- Create an attractive poster displaying the following:
    o Whether you owned a preferred seat, and for how long you maintained ownership.
    o Your total earnings (from Earnings Statements).
    o A one- or two-paragraph summary explaining the strategies you used to increase your total assets.
    o A one- or two-paragraph summary reflecting on your experience as a citizen of Ecopolis. Be sure to mention the greatest challenge that you faced.

Name: _____ Date: _____

ECONOMICS POSTASSESSMENT

Place your answers to the following questions in the boxes on the right.

1. Economics is the study of:
   A. How to produce goods.
   B. How to make decisions on spending.
   C. How society decides what, how, and for whom to produce goods and services.
   D. How to run our country.

   ☐

2. Economic resources are:
   A. Things like water and clean air.
   B. Items available for producing goods that satisfy human wants.
   C. Dependent on tastes and preferences of the population.
   D. The living standard in our society.

   ☐

3. A basic economic problem is that resources are:
   A. Too expensive.
   B. Able to be used for many things.
   C. Able to be combined to produce a commodity.
   D. Scarce.

   ☐

4. In a free market economy:
   A. Prices adjust upward or downward depending on how scarce goods are.
   B. The government decides how much goods will cost.
   C. The government decides which goods will be produced.
   D. Free goods are given away at the supermarket.

   ☐

5. The opportunity cost of a good is:
   A. The value of something else that is passed up when a
   B. good or service is bought.
   C. The amount of money spent on a product.
   D. The interest we get at a bank.
   E. The amount of time we spend shopping.

   ☐

6. When two goods can be used for the same purpose, they are said to be:
   A. A good bargain.
   B. Good for the economy.
   C. In demand.
   D. Substitutes.

7. The demand for a good can change if:
   A. I get a raise.
   B. The price of everything else goes up.
   C. There is a change in consumers' tastes and preferences.
   D. All of the above.

8. To economize means to:
   A. Study economics.
   B. Do the best you can with what you have.
   C. Save as much money as possible.
   D. Not buy anything.

9. On a graph, the demand curve:
   A. Moves downward as it goes to the right.
   B. Is the vertical axis.
   C. Moves upward as it goes to the right.
   D. Usually appears in red.

10. A characteristic of economic "wants" is that:
    A. They are necessary for existence.
    B. They are the same in all cultures.
    C. They can never be fully satisfied.
    D. They can be classified as labor or capital.

COMPLETE THE STATEMENTS

1. The difference between a need and a want is . . .

   _____

   _____

   _____

   _____

2. An example of an opportunity cost I experienced in Ecopolis is . . .

   _____

   _____

   _____

   _____

3. I couldn't get everything I wanted, so I chose to . . .

   _____

   _____

   _____

   _____

4. It was difficult developing a product or service because . . .

   _____

   _____

   _____

   _____

5. The hardest thing about being a leader is . . .

   _____

   _____

   _____

   _____

6. If preferred seating is imported, it creates a messy situation in Ecopolis because . . .

_____

_____

_____

_____

7. There was scarcity in Ecopolis. A few examples are . . .

_____

_____

_____

_____

8. We would have been better off if resources had been used to . . .

_____

_____

_____

_____

Appendix
Student Context Rubric

The Student Context Rubric (SCR) is intended for use by the classroom teacher as a tool to help in the identification of students of masked potential. This term, *masked potential*, refers to students who are gifted, but are frequently not identified because their behaviors are not displayed to best advantage by traditional methods. The SCR was designed to be used with this series of units and the authentic performance assessments that accompany them. Although you may choose to run the units without using the SCR, you may find the rubric helpful for keeping records of student behaviors.

The units serve as platforms for the display of student behaviors, while the SCR is an instrument that teachers can use to record those behaviors when making observations. The rubric requires the observer to record the frequency of gifted behaviors, but there is also the option to note that the student demonstrates the behavior with particular intensity. In this way, the rubric is subjective and requires careful observation and consideration.

It is recommended that an SCR be completed for each student prior to the application of a unit, and once again upon completion of the unit. In this way, teachers will be reminded of behaviors to look for during the unit—particularly those behaviors that we call *loophole behaviors*, which may indicate giftedness but are often misinterpreted or overlooked. (For instance, a student's verbal ability can be missed if he or she uses it to spin wild lies about having neglected to complete an assignment.) Therefore, the SCR allows teachers to be aware of—and to document—high-ability behavior even if it is masked or used in nontraditional ways. The mechanism also provides a method for tracking changes in teachers' perceptions of their students, not only while students are working on the Interactive Discovery-Based Units for High-Ability Learners, but also while they are engaged in traditional classroom activities.

In observing student behaviors, you might consider some of the following questions after completing a lesson:

- Was there anyone or anything that surprised you today?
- Did a particular student jump out at you today?
- Did someone come up with a unique or unusual idea today?
- Was there a moment in class today when you saw a lightbulb go on? Did it involve an individual, a small group, or the class as a whole?
- In reviewing written responses after a class discussion, were you surprised by anyone (either because he or she was quiet during the discussion but had good written ideas, or because he or she was passionate in the discussion but did not write with the same passion)?
- Did any interpersonal issues affect the classroom today? If so, how were these issues resolved?
- Did the lesson go as planned today? Were there any detours?
- Is there a student whom you find yourself thinking or worrying about outside of school?
- Are there students in your classroom who seem to be on a rollercoaster of learning—"on" one day, but "off" the next?
- Are your students different outside of the classroom? In what ways are they different?
- Are there students who refuse to engage with the project?
- During a class performance, did the leadership of a group change when students got in front of their peers?
- Did your students generate new ideas today?
- What was the energy like in your class today? Did you provide the energy, or did the students?
- How long did it take the students to engage today?

Ideally, multiple observers complete the SCR for each student. If a gifted and talented specialist is available, we recommend that he or she assist. By checking off the appropriate marks to describe student behaviors, and by completing the scoring chart, participants generate quantifiable data that can be used in advocating for students who would benefit from scaffolded services. **In terms of students' scores on the SCR, we do not provide concrete cutoffs or point requirements regarding which students should be recommended for special services.** Rather, the SCR is intended to flag students for scaffolded services and to enable them to reach their potential. It also provides a way to monitor and record students' behaviors.

What follows is an explanation of the categories and items included on the SCR, along with some examples of how the specified student behaviors might be evidenced in your classroom.

Engagement

1. **Student arrives in class with new ideas to bring to the project that he or she has thought of outside of class.** New ideas may manifest themselves as ideas about how to approach a problem, about new research information found on the Internet or elsewhere outside of class, about something in the news or in the paper that is relevant to the subject, or about a connection between the subject and an observed behavior.

2. **Student shares ideas with a small group of peers, but may fade into the background in front of a larger group.** The student may rise to be a leader when the small group is working on a project, but if asked to get up in front of the class, then that student fades into the background and lets others do the talking.

3. **Student engagement results in a marked increase in the quality of his or her performance.** This is particularly evident in a student who does not normally engage in class at all. During the unit, the student suddenly becomes engaged and produces something amazing.

4. **Student eagerly interacts with appropriate questions, but may be reluctant to put things down on paper.** This is an example of a loophole behavior, or one that causes a student to be overlooked when teachers and specialists are identifying giftedness. It is particularly evident in students who live in largely "oral" worlds, which is to say that they communicate best verbally and are often frustrated by written methods, or in those who have writing disabilities.

Creativity

1. **Student intuitively makes "leaps" in his or her thinking.** Occasionally, you will be explaining something, and a lightbulb will go on for a student, causing him or her to take the concept far beyond the content being covered. Although there are students who do this with regularity, it is more often an intensity behavior, meaning that when it occurs, the student is very intense in his or her thinking, creativity, reasoning, and so on. This can be tricky to identify, because often, the student is unable to explain his or her thinking, and the teacher realizes only later that a leap in understanding was achieved.

2. **Student makes up new rules, words, or protocols to express his or her own ideas.** This can take various forms, one of which is a student's taking two words and literally combining them to try to express what he or she is thinking about. Other times, a student will want to change the rules to make his or her idea possible.

3. **Student thinks on his or her feet in response to a project challenge, to make excuses, or to extend his or her work.** This is another loophole

behavior, because it often occurs when a student is being defensive or even misbehaving, making a teacher less likely to interpret it as evidence of giftedness. It is sometimes on display during classroom debates and discussions.

4. **Student uses pictures or other inventive means to illustrate his or her ideas.** Given the choice, this student would rather draw an idea than put it into words. This could take the shape of the student creating a character web or a design idea. The student might also act out an idea or use objects to demonstrate understanding.

Synthesis

1. **Student goes above and beyond directions to expand ideas.** It is wonderful to behold this behavior in students, particularly when displayed by those students who are rarely engaged. A student may be excited about a given idea and keep generating increasingly creative or complex material to expand upon that idea. For instance, we had a student who, during the mock trial unit, became intrigued by forensic evidence and decided to generate and interpret evidence to bolster his team's case.

2. **Student has strong opinions on projects, but may struggle to accept directions that contradict his or her opinions.** This student may understand directions, but be unwilling to yield to an idea that conflicts with his or her own idea. This behavior, rather than indicating a lack of understanding, is typical of students with strong ideas.

3. **Student is comfortable processing new ideas.** This behavior is evident in students who take new ideas and quickly extend them or ask insightful questions.

4. **Student blends new and old ideas.** This behavior has to do with processing a new idea, retrieving an older idea, and relating the two to one another. For instance, a student who learns about using string to measure distance might remember making a treasure map and extrapolate that a string would have been useful for taking into account curves and winding paths.

Interpersonal Ability

1. **Student is an academic leader who, when engaged, increases his or her levels of investment and enthusiasm in the group.** This is a student who has so much enthusiasm for learning that he or she makes the project engaging for the whole group, fostering an attitude of motivation or optimism.

2. **Student is a social leader in the classroom, but may not be an academic leader.** To observe this type of behavior, you may have to be vigilant, for some students are disengaged in the classroom but come alive as soon as they cross the threshold into the hallway, where they can socialize with their

peers. Often, this student is able to get the rest of the group to do whatever he or she wants (and does not necessarily use this talent for good).

3. **Student works through group conflict to enable the group to complete its work.** When the group has a conflict, this is the student who solves the problem or addresses the issue so that the group can get back to work. This is an interpersonal measure, and thus, it does not describe a student who simply elects to do all of the work rather than confronting his or her peers about sharing the load.

4. **Student is a Tom Sawyer in classroom situations, using his or her charm to get others to do the work.** There is an important distinction to watch out for when identifying this type of behavior: You must be sure that the student is *not* a bully, coercing others to do his or her work. Instead, this student actually makes other students *want* to lend a helping hand. For instance, a twice-exceptional student who is highly talented but struggles with reading might develop charm in order to get other students to transpose his verbally expressed ideas into writing.

Verbal Communication

1. **Participation in brainstorming sessions (e.g., group work) increases student's productivity.** When this type of student is given the opportunity to verbally process with peers, he or she is often able to come up with the answer. For instance, if asked outright for an answer, this student may shrug, but if given a minute to consult with a neighbor, then the student usually is able and willing to offer the correct answer.

2. **Student constructively disagrees with peers and/or the teacher by clearly sharing his or her thoughts.** This student can defend his or her point of view with examples and reasoning—not just in a formal debate, but also in general classroom situations. He or she has learned to channel thoughts into constructive disagreement, rather than flying off the handle merely to win an argument.

3. **Student verbally expresses his or her academic and/or social needs.** This student can speak up when confused or experiencing personality clashes within a group. This student knows when to ask for help and can clearly articulate what help is needed.

4. **Student uses strong word choice and a variety of tones to bring expression to his or her verbal communication.** This student is an engaging speaker and speaks loudly and clearly enough for everybody to hear. A wide vocabulary is also indicative that this student's verbal capability is exceptional.

Student: _____

Date: _____

Fill out the rubric according to what you have observed about each student's behaviors. Then, for each area, record the number of items you marked "Not observed," "Sometimes," and "Often." Multiply these tallies by the corresponding point values (0, 1, and 2) to get the totals for each area. There is an option to check for high intensity so you can better keep track of students' behaviors.

STUDENT CONTEXT RUBRIC

ENGAGEMENT

1. Student arrives in class with new ideas to bring to the project that he or she has thought of outside of class.
   NOT OBSERVED   SOMETIMES   OFTEN   HIGH INTENSITY

2. Student shares ideas with a small group of peers, but may fade into the background in front of a larger group.
   NOT OBSERVED   SOMETIMES   OFTEN   HIGH INTENSITY

3. Student engagement results in a marked increase in the quality of his or her performance.
   NOT OBSERVED   SOMETIMES   OFTEN   HIGH INTENSITY

4. Student eagerly interacts with appropriate questions, but may be reluctant to put things down on paper.
   NOT OBSERVED   SOMETIMES   OFTEN   HIGH INTENSITY

CREATIVITY

1. Student intuitively makes "leaps" in his or her thinking.
   NOT OBSERVED   SOMETIMES   OFTEN   HIGH INTENSITY

2. Student makes up new rules, words, or protocols to express his or her own ideas.
   NOT OBSERVED   SOMETIMES   OFTEN   HIGH INTENSITY

3. Student thinks on his or her feet in response to a project challenge, to make excuses, or to extend his or her work.
   NOT OBSERVED   SOMETIMES   OFTEN   HIGH INTENSITY

4. Student uses pictures or other inventive means to illustrate his or her ideas.
   NOT OBSERVED   SOMETIMES   OFTEN   HIGH INTENSITY

SYNTHESIS

1. Student goes above and beyond directions to expand ideas.
   NOT OBSERVED   SOMETIMES   OFTEN   HIGH INTENSITY

2. Student has strong opinions on projects, but may struggle to accept directions that contradict his or her opinions.
   NOT OBSERVED   SOMETIMES   OFTEN   HIGH INTENSITY

3. Student is comfortable processing new ideas.
   NOT OBSERVED   SOMETIMES   OFTEN   HIGH INTENSITY

4. Student blends new ideas and old ideas.
   NOT OBSERVED   SOMETIMES   OFTEN   HIGH INTENSITY

INTERPERSONAL ABILITY

1. Student is an academic leader who, when engaged, increases his or her levels of investment and enthusiasm in the group.
   NOT OBSERVED   SOMETIMES   OFTEN   HIGH INTENSITY

2. Student is a social leader in the classroom, but may not be an academic leader.
   NOT OBSERVED   SOMETIMES   OFTEN   HIGH INTENSITY

3. Student works through group conflict to enable the group to complete its work.
   NOT OBSERVED   SOMETIMES   OFTEN   HIGH INTENSITY

4. Student is a Tom Sawyer in classroom situations, using his or her charm to get others to do the work.
   NOT OBSERVED   SOMETIMES   OFTEN   HIGH INTENSITY

VERBAL COMMUNICATION

1. Participation in brainstorming sessions (e.g., group work) increases student's productivity.
   NOT OBSERVED   SOMETIMES   OFTEN   HIGH INTENSITY

2. Student constructively disagrees with peers and/or the teacher by clearly sharing his or her thoughts.
   NOT OBSERVED   SOMETIMES   OFTEN   HIGH INTENSITY

3. Student verbally expresses his or her academic and/or social needs.
   NOT OBSERVED   SOMETIMES   OFTEN   HIGH INTENSITY

4. Student uses strong word choice and a variety of tones to bring expression to his or her verbal communication.
   NOT OBSERVED   SOMETIMES   OFTEN   HIGH INTENSITY

AREA	NOT 0	SOME 1	OFTEN 2	HIGH	TOTAL
ENGAGEMENT					
CREATIVITY					
SYNTHESIS					
INTERPERSONAL ABILITY					
VERBAL COMMUNICATION					
ADD TOTALS					

Developed by Cote & Blauvelt under the auspices of the Further Steps Forward Project, a Jacob K. Javits grant program, #S206A050086.

Ecopolis © Prufrock Press Inc.

About the Authors

Richard G. Cote, M.B.A., is a career educator. He has dedicated 41 years to being a classroom teacher (mathematics, physics), a community college adjunct instructor (economics), a gifted and talented resource specialist, and the director of the Further Steps Forward Project, funded under Javits legislation.

His development of the MESH (mathematics, English, science, and history) program has led him to several audiences. He has presented at various national conventions, civic/community groups, district school boards, teacher organizations, community colleges, and universities and has served as a consultant to educators throughout the country. Cote helped develop the teacher certification examination for physics at the Institute for Educational Testing and Research at the University of South Florida. He completed the Florida Council on Educational Management Program in Educational Leadership, and he is the recipient of numerous awards, including a certificate of merit on economics education from the University of South Florida, a grant from the Florida Council on Economics Education, a Florida Compact award, and a prestigious NAGC Curriculum Studies award for the development of *Ecopolis* and *What's Your Opinion?*

Now retired from the workplace, Cote continues to share his energy, creativity, and expertise with educators through the Interactive Discovery-Based Units for High-Ability Learners.

Darcy O. Blauvelt has been teaching in a variety of facilities for more than 12 years. Her educational journey has included public schools, private schools, nursery schools, and a professional theatre for children ages 3–18. Blauvelt holds educational certification in Theatre K–12, Early Childhood Education, and English Education 5–12. She holds a B.A. in theatre from Chatham College, Pittsburgh, PA, and has done graduate work at Lesley University, MA, in creative arts in learning, as well as at Millersville University, PA, in psychology.

In 2005, she joined the Nashua School District as a gifted and talented resource specialist. Subsequently, she served full time as the program coordinator for the Further Steps Forward Project, a Javits Grant program, from 2005–2009. Blauvelt returned to the classroom in the fall of 2009 and currently teaches seventh-grade English in Nashua, NH. Blauvelt lives in Manchester, NH, with her husband, two dogs, five cats, and the occasional son!